61 Minutes

Reflections and Homilies for the Year of Luke

Rev. Michael W. Rothan
Roman Catholic Diocese of Harrisburg

authorHOUSE®

AuthorHouse™
1663 Liberty Drive
Bloomington, IN 47403
www.authorhouse.com
Phone: 1-800-839-8640

First published by AuthorHouse 11/11/2009

ISBN: 978-1-4490-2029-3 (e)
ISBN: 978-1-4490-2028-6 (sc)

Library of Congress Control Number: 2009911378

Printed in the United States of America
Bloomington, Indiana

This book is printed on acid-free paper.

The photo on the cover is a stained glass window at St. Benedict the Abbot Church, Lebanon Pennsylvania. Taken at dusk.

And his mother kept all these things in her heart…

~Luke 2: 51

For the Brothers and Priests
at St. Vincent Seminary in Latrobe,
who taught me what I needed to know
in order to be a good priest.

For my brother Priests
in the Diocese of Harrisburg,
both living and deceased:
examples to me of faith, brotherhood and
the goodness of our God.

Contents

FORWARD

How very appropriate that during this Year of Priests as proclaimed by our Holy Father, Pope Benedict XVI, Father Rothan, one of our outstanding Diocesan Priests, offer us his Second Edition of *"61 Minutes"* by sharing with us his insightful and inspirational Sunday homilies for the "C" cycle. During the ordinary time of this liturgical year, the Evangelist, Saint Luke, will be our herald, who himself offers us the Gospel message without compromise. Throughout the pages of his Gospel, Saint Luke gives special recognition to the poor and to women; and he gives honor to and focuses upon in a unique way Mary, Our Lady, the Most Holy Mother of God.

At this time in the history of our Church, Pope Benedict invites our universal Catholic Church to recall with gratitude the sterling example of the life of Saint John Vianney, whose 150th anniversary of birth into life eternal we commemorate this year. As well, our own Bishop Rhoades is proclaiming throughout our Diocese, this very year October 2009-2010, a Jubilee Year in honor of Mary, our spiritual Mother.

The fact that these proclamations are called forth by Pope Benedict XVI and by Bishop Rhoades at the very same time that Father Rothan releases this new edition, is not, by any means a coincidence, but rather, is truly Divine Providence in my humble estimation.

This collection of reflective homilies does not demand a lengthy forward because they continue the style of a homilist who himself has been richly inspired by the solid faith lives of so many, most especially Our Blessed Mother and Saint John Vianney, the Curé of Ars.

The powerful homilies contained within this edition reveal for us, in a more concrete way, how authentically preaching the Word of God can, and indeed does, delight, excite, thrill, challenge and even convert, not only individual souls themselves, but also entire congregations too.

I encourage you to prayerfully go through these pages and allow your soul to be spiritually enriched and nourished so that you too, will authentically preach the message of the Holy Word of God each and every day, by the very way in which you live your daily life, without ever having to speak one word.

Mary, Holy Mother of God, *pray for us!*

Saint John Vianney, *pray for us!*

Saint Luke the Evangelist, *pray for us!*

> Reverend Louis P. Ogden, Pastor
>
> Seven Sorrows of the Blessed Virgin Mary Parish
>
> Middletown, Pennsylvania
>
> 9 June 2009
>
> Solemnity of the Most Sacred Heart of Jesus

INTRODUCTION

I know it's the same title as the last one! Cut me some slack, will ya! I had just sat down and was beginning to enjoy the published work, and then some emails came around, and then some book signings and then some calls. I don't know how to respond to the statements really, because they weren't negative; on the contrary, they were very positive. But most of the statements were similar to each other. Three statements made their way to my ears on more than one occasion. The first is one of the greatest compliments I could have received: "I can hear you speaking when I read the book." Great. Never mind my grammatical errors or rough speech and colloquialisms, it was accepted as a spoken text. Others would complement the book and say, "I liked it so much that I didn't wait from week to week, but read the whole thing." That's a fine statement, but it usually had another clause attached: "When's the next one coming out?"

Well, needless to say, that was a little disappointing for two reasons: the first is that they did just what I didn't want them to and read through the whole thing, while the goal was to get people to slow down...reflect on the scriptures...come up with their own reflection and then read mine. The second reason is...I felt pressure now to offer a second installment. So here it is!

The title of this book is "61 minutes". We are all called, as priests, to make a holy hour, or spend 60 minutes in front of the Blessed Sacrament, in the presence of God each day. I would find myself praying for maybe fifty minutes, and I would receive nothing in the way of inspiring thoughts or insights. Because I wasn't getting anything, I would be tempted to leave early. But if I stayed, I found over time that it was usually the fifty-eighth or fifty-ninth minute that God chose to enlighten me. I had to be faithful. Is it any wonder that Jesus asked the apostles in the garden to stay awake with him and pray? So now, just to make sure I give God all the time He needs, I make my holy hour 61 minutes. Just in case!

Yep, it's the same title. In fact that last paragraph was cut and pasted from the other book. Some people were suggesting new titles: "62 minutes"; "another 61 minutes"; "over an hour", etc. I decided to remain with the same title, because in principle it is the same. The only thing that has changed with my holy hour is the time of day. I started making a holy hour at night. Judging by the Jewish way of keeping time, that is the beginning of the next day anyway. Instead of beginning in the dark and leaving as the sun is breaking over the horizon, I now begin my holy hour with the dusky glow through the stained glass, and end in the darkness of night.

The change from morning to night is apropos to this composition. This book focuses on the year of Luke. Luke's gospel uses some of the most eloquent Greek prose you will read (provided you can read Greek) and so I really try to delve into the original language of the text. The beauty of the language is overshadowed, however, by the story of the Christ as the fulfillment of the Old Testament.

Luke begins this first volume stating very clearly what he wants to do: *to write an orderly account for you…that you may know the truth concerning the things of which you have been informed* (Luke 1: 3-4). He wants to show us *why* we should believe, and *what*, we have to hope for. His gospel is often called the Gospel of women, of the poor, and of prayer. Not a few times do we see Jesus going off to pray by himself, and most often it occurs right as the crimson sun sinks into the horizon. These hours comprise part of the hidden life of Jesus as well. These were hours of communion with his Father, during which he gained strength for the tests that would come.

I would be remiss if I didn't mention the Mother of Jesus. She and I have come a long way in the last ten years. I never really thought too much about Mary, and certainly never had a devotion to her, until I entered the Seminary. I began to have a certain devotion to her, but then was *put off* by the *Mariolatry* I witnessed in some seminarians and priests, and the discrimination I felt from others because I was not so devout. That really drove me away from her for quite some time, in fact most of my five years at the seminary. It was only when I began to see her as the young scared youth who was not afraid to say yes, that I found my patroness. A mother who embraced me as though I had never left. I have a very strong devotion to our Lady, and although we have very little spoken about her scripturally, most of what is said, occurs in this Gospel.

There are a few changes to the book, in comparison to the first installment. I encourage you, once again, to read the passages for the Sunday <u>on your own first</u>. I have included in this edition all the readings from scripture at the top of the page, and have added the Psalm as well. The Psalms are sometimes ignored or skipped over, and yet they are such a rich source of reflection and prayer. Jacques Trublet asks how it came to be that the psalms, which represent only 6.4 percent of the Old Testament, make up a quarter of all the New Testament's citations from the Old Testament.[1] When the scriptures are used in the text of the homily, they are written in italics. In the appendices, I have included homilies from some days which are holy, but not holy days of obligation. I have also included homilies I presented to high school students at both Trinity High School in Camp Hill, and Lebanon Catholic School.

I hope now, I will be left alone for awhile as far as publications are concerned! Just kidding, ha ha (no I'm not). In all seriousness, though, my greatest desire is that these reflections might help to draw you closer to the God who created you from the beginning when He could've created anyone else; and continues to invite you to commune with Him, much as Christ did centuries ago in the middle of the fertile crescent along the sea of Galilee. And perhaps as Mary, it may give you things…to keep in the stillness of your heart. Enjoy! Read, Re-Read, underline and teach!

Rev. Michael W. Rothan

Written at hermitage *Pangaea*

18 June 2009

---

1 Jacques Trublet in William M. Thompson, The Struggle for Theology's Soul: Contesting Scripture in Christology, (New York: Crossroad Publishing Co., 1996), 45.

First Sunday of Advent

Jeremiah 33: 14-16; 1 Thess. 3:12-4:2; Luke 21: 25-28, 34-36 Psalm 25

What are you running on?

What if one breath was all we needed for life? Years could pass, and all we would require is one breath? (It'd be some pretty bad breath probably). What if all we needed was one drink for our life; our whole life? What if we only needed to eat one meal and we would be nourished forever? I don't know how many of you would like that, but I know I surely would not! We are living beings, not some sort of inanimate thing; so we need a constant supply of air, food, and drink. We don't question this, because we are made in such a way that if we go without any of these things, our bodies will protest. Why then, do we presume that a minimal amount of spirituality will suffice for life? Why do we presume that a prayer said once a year; once a week; or even once a day is enough? We eat, drink, and breathe several times a day. We need those things for our physical existence... but what about our spiritual existence?

Listen to Jeremiah: *The days are coming, says the LORD, when I will fulfill the promise I made to the house of Israel and Judah.* **I will fulfill**, means not fulfilled yet! It means that in this life our spiritual self is shadowed by our bodies which need constant nourishment. Jesus warns: *Beware that your hearts do not become drowsy from carousing and drunkenness and the anxieties of daily life, and that day catch you by surprise like a trap.*

We have that empty pit, that grumbling in our stomachs when we are hungry; and that dry mouth when thirsty; we are out of breath or must rest when we are not breathing well. But perhaps there's that other ache...that other emptiness; that *something* that is missing, and we haven't been able to put our finger on it. So we've bought things for ourselves and others; we've read books or begun programs, and yet nothing seems to help. What is *THAT* yearning pointing to?

> A guy's car was broken down on the side of the road. A tow truck came along and hauled him to the garage. They worked for hours on the car, trying to determine what the problem was. The mechanic tried an air filter, oil change, all the basic stuff, but to no avail. Then it got more expensive. He began to take the engine apart and rebuild it; put in new spark plugs and a starter, but still nothing happened. This last visit the man was ready to take the car to the junkyard, so he brought his son along. His son said: "Daddy, is your car out of gas?" The two reluctantly checked the tank and sure enough, it was dry as a bone. They filled the tank and the car started up…a couple thousand dollars later.[2]

Sometimes, we need to stop attempting to fix the problem by putting in new parts, or trying new experiences, and look at the obvious. Is the tank empty? Has it *been* empty? Before you throw away the whole thing, check what's in the tank. Let this be an opportunity to fill it with fuel for the journey; and we will be well on our way to satisfying that hunger that God placed in our hearts from the very beginning.

---

2 Paraphrased from a story by Charles Allen Kollar, *Solution-Focused Pastoral Counseling: An Effective Short-Term Approach for Getting People Back on Track*, (Grand Rapids, MI: Zondervan, 1997), 71.

Second Sunday of Advent

Baruch 5:1-9; Philippians 1:4-6, 8-11; Luke 3:1-6; Psalm 126

What are WE celebrating?

Paul writes to the Philippians*: And this is my prayer: that your love may increase ever more and more in knowledge and every kind of perception, to discern what is of value, so that you may be pure and blameless for the day of Christ, filled with the fruit of righteousness that comes through Jesus Christ for the glory and praise of God.*

Have you received your cards yet? Gotten all your packages and food and *knick knacks* ready for Christmas? I guarantee you, many shoppers started weeks ago…maybe months ago. My aunt and uncle in Kentucky just leave their decorations up all year long; that way they don't have to put them away, just replace a bulb now and then. How long have we saved? The culmination of hours of work and stress and toil; tackling to get the last "Web-Kin"; camped outside of the stores, so that when the doors open, and they offer the "hundred free laptops," I'll be able to get one. We are the ones fighting our way through countless children and forcing our child ahead of us, who is petrified to sit on Santa's lap, for the picture they will one day cherish…a picture of their horror at being so placed. This is what we celebrate…right? What does it mean to celebrate?

Of all of the definitions for "celebrate" in Oxford's, three out of the five are these: Make publicly known; perform a religious rite; preside at (the Eucharist). "People do not have to believe what we say, but they will believe what we do."[3] What ARE we celebrating? Perhaps in order to really say what it *is*, we have to look at it from the other seat.

---

3 Anonymous.

As difficult as it is, imagine for a moment that you do not believe in God…that you are an unbeliever. Then answer these questions: If you do not believe in God, what do you celebrate when everyone else is celebrating Christmas? All we need to do is find some toddlers and most will tell you, "Gifts, Santa, food, stockings." No? If we do not believe in God, then when everyone else is celebrating Easter, what do we do? "We celebrate the Easter Bunny, colored eggs, candy, and spring." If we do not believe in God, when everyone else is celebrating the memorial of St. Valentine's Day, what do we do? "Send cards, candy, flowers, to our loved ones." When we are celebrating one of the holiest days of the year, All Saints Day, if we don't believe in God and have no concept of the saints what do we celebrate? The night before…All Saints Eve, or Hallows Eve. Do you see a trend here?

The believer commemorates all these feasts in homage to God. We sacrifice, have special Liturgies, and make offerings to God. Such is not the case with the world that does not believe in God. "The world, is not satisfied with simply ignoring God but is seeking to destroy God, and wishes that God was not."[4] The world that denies God, designs these counterparts which take focus away from God and place it on the *self*.

Take notice, that for the Christian counterparts, the homage, gifts, words, etc. do not go to God, but to us. And ironically, each of these "feasts" necessarily requires us to buy something. There is the clincher. You have noticed I am sure, that many of the stores began decorating for Christmas long before the beginning of Advent, let alone the beginning of November. I wonder if they would be so zealous if they had nothing to sell? Why do they not decorate for our other major feasts, like the Ascension, Pentecost, the Assumption? Why do the decorations come down so quickly the day after Christmas? Hmmm.

This year, you will recall that many stores did not open at dawn on "Black Friday" but opened at 12 a.m. the night before. How many do you think showed up at midnight? (Perhaps you know because you were there!) Enough that the news crews were there. How many

---

4 Bishop Fulton J. Sheen, Lift Up Your Heart, (New York: McGraw-Hill, 1950), 51.

of them do you think will show up for midnight Mass? How many do you think will get up for Mass at Dawn? Perhaps that would be inconvenient. In the South, and even some places in the North, non-Catholic Churches are closing on Christmas Day. I know it sounds ludicrous, but they say that people should be with their families on Christmas, and that worship would be inconvenient. I wonder what *they* will celebrate.

The prophet says: *Stand upon the heights; look to the east and see your children gathered from the east and the west at the word of the Holy One...* Will *our* children be gathered at the word of the holy one? Thinking not like Godless people but as believers, ask yourself this question: "Would we celebrate Christmas as we do, if Santa decided not to come this year? Would we celebrate Christmas as we do, if there were going to be no presents this year? I find it very interesting that in some third-world countries, they will have no presents this year or even a special meal, if they eat at all. But they will celebrate the birth of Christ, and what a celebration it will be. I am told by my priest friend in Uganda that the Mass lasts half a day! So much for complaining about the Easter Vigil!

A voice of one crying out in the desert: *Prepare the way of the Lord, make straight his paths.* Perhaps just a voice crying out in the desert. When all is said and done; when the cards are sent; gifts wrapped; all the food ready to go and we begin to go over our list and see if there is anything we forgot, take a look in the manger; and perhaps, there we will see what's been missing for quite some time.

Feast of the Immaculate Conception (See Appendix I)

Third Sunday of Advent

Zephaniah 3:14-18; Philippians 4:4-7; Luke 3:10-18; (Isaiah 12)[5]

A debt that can never be repaid.

We hear a lot about redemption in the scriptures, in our books on theology and even in homilies (imagine that!). But what does that really mean? I mean, come on, it's nice language, and makes us feel good about being a Christian, let alone a Catholic, but can we really understand what that means in the here and now? I thought it was interesting that when the word comes up in scripture, it's associated with one person: Christ. So who is the *Redeemer*, and what is *redemption* to us?

If I offered $1000.00 to a rich woman, or a homeless woman, who would appreciate it more? If I offered to perform plastic surgery on a burn victim or a model, who would realize the benefits more. If I could give a full college scholarship to a person who was least likely to succeed, or offer it to the valedictorian at a local high school, who would appreciate it more? Certainly we realize that those who would react most gratefully in any of these circumstances are those who are least likely to experience them. Therefore, when the seeming "wish for one in a million" comes true, they are also the most grateful.

---

5 Isaiah 12: 2-5 is used instead of a Psalm for the Responsorial. When this occurs the passage is in parentheses.

The same is true of our redemption. To redeem means to "buy back." *Apolutrōsen* is the word in Greek. It comes from the Greek word *Lutron* which was a ransom paid to free someone condemned to die.[6] But wait…can a judge pay the ransom for the one he has also convicted? John the Baptizer says: *His winnowing-fan is in his hand to clear his threshing floor and gather the wheat into his granary, but the chaff, he will burn.* The chaff consists of the husks which are so light they can be blown about by the wind. It speaks of one with no direction; perhaps one which desires no direction but their own. How can we speak of redemption, when the winnowing fan is in hand? Because the Judge, also happens to be the savior.

The prophet Zephaniah says: *Shout for joy, O daughter Zion! Sing joyfully, O Israel! Be glad and exult with all your heart, O daughter Jerusalem! The Lord has removed the judgment against you… The Lord God is in your midst, a mighty savior.* A Savior! A Redeemer!

There is a story of a boy who wanted a sailboat to play with in the river. His dad told him he would have to save up his money to buy one, because his birthday had already passed. The boy wasn't about to save up money, so with his father's help, he decided to make one. They cut out the main body together and then the boy sanded it down, and put in the details with his pen knife. He painted it, made a mast and sail and it was really beautiful to behold. It almost looked professional. The first day he took it down to the river, the river was high. He let the boat go free on the bank with the intention of being able to recapture it downstream, but with the water so swift, it quickly took the boat away. All that time… all that energy, and the boat was gone. The boy grieved the loss, after all that work.

Days later he was walking by a toy shop in town, and low and behold, there in the window was his boat! He ran into the shop and asked the man to see the boat. The man, thinking he had a sale, offered it to the boy. The boy looked up and said: "Yep, this is my boat alright. I remember doing all this work." The man

---

6 *Enhanced Strong's Lexicon*, (Oak Harbor, WA: Logos Research Systems, Inc., 1995), *Lutron*.

looked doubtful. "Sorry son, that's my boat. You may buy it if you want." Although the boy argued, the man would not relent. So he told the boy what it cost and offered to sell it to him. The boy worked hard the next few days to get enough money to buy the boat. Finally, he walked to the store and handed the money to the shopkeeper, who gave him the boat. As he walked down the street clutching the boat in his hands he whispered softly to it: "Now you are twice mine. Twice, because I first created you; you went away; and now I have bought you back![7]

This is the joy of redemption! Many of us are like the chaff driven by any breeze that comes our way. Redemption, however, requires work on our part. It requires our desire to allow the Creator to direct our course. The *Judge*, casts a verdict based on what we do, or do not. And yet if we desire to change, even amidst our mistakes in the past, He pays the ransom. Then, we are twice his, and we can experience the joy that comes with redemption. The joy for the purchaser who has redeemed his creation, and for the creature who has been reunited with the Creator.

---

7 Internet Forward.

Fourth Sunday of Advent

Micah 5: 1-4; Hebrews 10:5-10; Luke 1: 39-45; Psalm 80

Keep Christ in Christ-mas

Looking at and reflecting upon the readings for today, I considered all the stories we have from Sacred Scripture. Have you ever really just sat down and considered all we have? The story from the prophet Micah about the great gift which shall come from the most unlikely place: a Ruler, whose origin was foretold from ancient times. The Letter to the Hebrews, describing the true sacrifice and offering God desires. And finally the Gospel story of a woman whose "yes" would change her life forever. This is real stuff! Imagine at the visitation, that even before these babies were born, the grace of their souls could be felt by each other! What a rich and wonderful tradition.

What amazes me most of all, is how everything they said and did; all they experienced, was seen and perceived through the lens of God. If they were happy or sad, it was God. If they were sick or healthy, it was God. When they ate, God was thanked, and when they went without, they offered the fast to God. Their life was centered around their faith. Not only on certain feasts of the year, but every single day, consecrated to God.

We have done the opposite. We have in many ways, made God an accessory, and an optional one at that. The world continues to encourage this attitude by distracting us from the most important things, with less important matters. This has pervaded our way of thinking so much, that even those feasts that we held so sacred in our lives, have now been reduced to simply a season of the secular year, or a time when we can expect sales to occur.

The following is a paraphrased statement, originally written by Ben Stein and recited by him on CBS Sunday Morning Commentary. Bear in mind that it is dated a bit, so the "Nick and Jessica" he is speaking of refers to Jessica Simpson and Nick Lachey, but you can substitute any couple or star in the blank at this point.[8]

Here with a few confessions from my beating heart: I have no freaking clue who Nick and Jessica are. I see them on the cover of *People* and *US* constantly when I am buying my dog biscuits and kitty litter. I often ask the checkers at the grocery stores. They never know who Nick and Jessica are either. Who are they? Will it change my life if I know who they are and why they have broken up? Why are they so important?

I don't know who Lindsay Lohan is either, and I do not care at all about Tom Cruise's wife. Am I going to be called before a Senate committee and asked if I am a subversive? Maybe, but I just have no clue who Nick and Jessica are. If this is what it means to be no longer young. It's not so bad.

Next confession: I am a Jew, and every single one of my ancestors was Jewish. And it does not bother me even a little bit when people call those beautiful lit up, bejeweled trees, Christmas trees. I don't feel threatened. I don't feel discriminated against. That's what they are: Christmas trees. It doesn't bother me a bit when people say, "Merry Christmas" to me. I don't think they are slighting me or getting ready to put me in a ghetto. In fact, I kind of like it. It shows that we are all brothers and sisters celebrating this happy time of year. It doesn't bother me at all that there is a manger scene on display at a key intersection near my beach house in Malibu. If people want a crèche, it's just as fine with me as is the Menorah a few hundred yards away.

I don't like getting pushed around for being a Jew, and I don't think Christians like getting pushed around for being Christians. I think people who believe in God are sick and tired of getting pushed around, period. I have no idea where the concept came

---

8 Internet Forward

from that America is an explicitly atheist country. I can't find it in the Constitution, and I don't like it being shoved down my throat. Or maybe I can put it another way: where did the idea come from that we should worship Nick and Jessica and we aren't allowed to worship God as we understand Him? I guess that's a sign that I'm getting old, too.

But there are a lot of us who are wondering where Nick and Jessica came from and where the America we knew went to. In light of the many jokes we send to one another for a laugh, this is a little different: This is not intended to be a joke; it's not funny, it's intended to get you thinking.

To recapture our spirit and offer to God what belongs to Him (which is everything), we need only want it bad enough. Imagine if we would consecrate our days, our hours, our minutes to the one who can help us the most. Imagine, perhaps if Nick and Jessica, or Tom Cruise and his wife did the same...perhaps we would not be reading about them anymore, or at least, not in the tabloids.

Christmas Homily
Mass at Dawn

Isaiah 62: 11-12; Titus 3:4-7; Luke 2: 15-20;
Psalm 97
(Cycle ABC)

I would like to tell you a story…

Once, many years ago, out in the west, what is called the dust bowl, there was a drought. For those of you who do not know what that is, it means there is no water. That there has not been rain in a very long time, and so everything begins to die. There were not good crops that year, and there were many dust storms. Such was the case in this little town, where the supply of water was quickly running out. In order to save water, each family was permitted only a small amount each day. So in one particular family, the father gave each person a small bucket. He gave one to his wife and his two daughters and his small four-year-old son. In this bucket, each day, he would put the amount of water they needed to last the whole day (which was not very much at all).

One day, the mother was at the window of the kitchen preparing the day's meal, when she saw her son. He had a cup in his hands and was walking very slowly and carefully, not to spill a single drop. As she continued to watch him, she saw him walk towards the woods, and then into the brush where she lost sight of him. About five minutes passed, and she was getting ready to go after him when he emerged from the brush. He was no longer walking carefully, but actually running, as though he had some purpose in mind.

She continued to observe him, and saw that he was taking his small bucket with just a bit of water and very carefully pouring it into the cup he was carrying (for the water wasn't nearly enough to dip the cup in the bucket). He then began his careful walk back into the woods. The mother was concerned that her son was wasting the water, making mud puddles or throwing it around. She immediately became incensed and as she was going to go after him, saw him once again return from the woods running with determination. At that moment, she decided to wait.

Once again, the child carefully poured the water from the small bucket into the cup, and then began his careful trek across the dry field into the forest. This time his mother followed at a distance, careful not to be seen. As he passed into the brush, she quietly speeded up a bit so she wouldn't lose track of him. She couldn't see him, but followed his footsteps in the dusty ground and then she gasped.

There must have been a dozen deer, forming a loosely connected circle. In the center was a large buck with six points on each antler. Beside him a doe who had her head lowered to the ground, gently nuzzling a tiny fawn…and at the feet of the doe was her son. He was kneeling down beside the small fawn who lay dying. Its tongue was out of its mouth and its breathing was labored. The boy was slowly and carefully holding the cup just close enough that the deer could slurp some water. With every sip, it appeared as if life was coming back into the fawn. The deer watched helplessly, as they allowed this human to save their fawn. A baby human, much like their fawn, who was giving his whole bucket; all the water he had, for the life of the deer; a deer that could do nothing for him in return. [9]

Boys and girls, *you* are that fawn. This is a Christmas story. *He* would come as a child and give everything he had for those who didn't even know him; for those who could give nothing back to him. Now.… what would've happened if the boy's mother had stopped him? What would've happened if the deer didn't drink? What would've happened

---

9 Internet Forward.

if the deer's parents didn't allow the fawn to drink, or they kept the boy from offering the water?

This is a Christmas story. You are the fawn. There was never a danger that the son would not offer the water. There was only one danger; the only danger that has ever been: that those around us might prevent us from drinking what *will* give us life; and that those who *can* drink refuse to do so. Boys and Girls, that is not the end of the story.

…As the boy finished giving the last of his water to the fawn, and the fawn staggered to his feet, a low rumble of thunder was heard, and then the skies opened up, and for the first time in months, it rained.

Feast of the Holy Family Sunday within the Octave of Christmas

Sirach 3:2-6, 12-14; Colossians 3:12-21; Luke 2: 41-52; Psalm 128

The Holy Family, is the one set apart.

I know a family, and I'll bet you've seen them. I met them at my first parish, and at first appearance, you might not even think they were a family. Every Sunday, without fail, they would cart the kids into the church: three boys and a girl. The night before, Paul was watching a show on "Jesus of Nazareth." On Sunday, he would not get out of bed for church. He kept saying that they didn't have to go. "What do you mean you don't have to go?" his mom replied. Paul said: "No, we don't have to go. He's dead, I saw it last night on TV."

You can imagine the effort it took every Sunday. But they would always make it to church. Before too long, either the father or mother would grab two of the kids and take them to the narthex of the church because of "disorderly conduct" while the other two remained. When they referred to this exercise, they called it, "the walk of shame."

It was fascinating to me that this couple would struggle week after week to come to Mass together, and then split up soon after arriving. Since then, they say it's gotten much better; however, I've been transferred since then, so I wouldn't know. I would propose, however, that their "walk of shame" was not so much a sign of *defeat*, as it was a sign of *fidelity*. How many others will not bring their children to Mass because it's too distracting, or they "can't sit still" or just because a small child is a nice excuse not to have to go? What was it Jesus said: *Let the little children come to me and do not hinder them; for the kingdom of God is made up of such as these.*

Picture it: Jesus and his parents are where? CHURCH! They went to the temple for the feast of Passover. (Needless to say when they went for Passover twenty years later it would not be as pleasant. Mary would lose Jesus again. This time the teachers would be interrogating him, as opposed to simply asking him questions in the temple area.) The place is a zoo...I mean literally. They would have the animals for the sacrifices, people would be with family and clan and tribe; there would be stories and reunions, all of this going on in the midst of Church!

See, a Holy Family is not one that is perfect; a holy family is not one without issues; but a holy family knows where they are fueled... they know from Whom they get their authority as parents, and with Whom they are to walk as children. I love how Sirach puts it: *The Lord sets a father in honor over his children; a mother's authority he confirms over her sons. [Therefore] He who honors his father atones for sins; he stores up riches who reveres his mother.*

As God created our souls, He scoured the universe looking for two souls with whom to entrust ours...and he chose our parents. Not because they were perfect or without defect; but because they had the possibility to be the best of parents. This feast is about a family who builds their love for each other after the love they had, first for God. And because their love of God was a true love, without expectation, their love for each other came very easily.

My sister Elaine and her husband David just gave birth to their sixth child, Michael Gabriel Romero. What a strong name! (And not just because it is my name as well.) Many people would respond, "What are you thinking?!" Their response is so much different from my own, and from that child's brothers and sisters. I am as ecstatic as they are about the birth of their new sibling, much as I imagine our Lord is whenever He gets to create a new soul. We have the capacity to be a holy family, if we can accept the gift of life God has entrusted to us, and find our source of life and goodness in Him.

EPIPHANY

ISAIAH 60: 1-6; EPHESIANS 3:2-3, 5-6; MATTHEW 2: 1-12; PSALM 72

"Wise men still seek Him."

I was at a party for New Years. Now, usually I wouldn't go to these things, but my brother-in-law and his friend were throwing it, so I thought the crowd would be like family for the most part (boy was I wrong…but anyway). I was watching the people dance and have a generally good time, when a gentleman (more or less) approached me and sat down. He was obviously "resting in the spirit" (or *spirits*) and asked if I was the guy who was a priest. I said I was, knowing that I had somehow been "outed" by one of my relatives or friends. Then he made a statement I've heard a million times: "I'm a spiritual person, I just don't go to Church."

This lead us into a discussion of what a "spiritual person" is (keeping in mind he had more of his share of "spirits" that evening.) He was asking questions and getting answers, but he might say he "was getting nowhere." Finally he said: "You're lucky I go to church twice a year." "I am lucky? I…am lucky? How does it affect me? It has nothing to do with me. Answer me this: would you tell the One who gave you your first breath this morning, He was lucky you went to Church? Would you stand in the presence of the One who has the power to give you another minute of life or an eternity of punishment 'He is lucky' because of something *you* do?"

He paused for a moment, obviously taken off guard and put his hand behind his head, revealing the gold medal he was wearing of the Sacred Heart. Then the real fun began. "Do you know who that is on your necklace? And although he knew *who* it was, he didn't know *what* it was. Many, many people say they are "spiritual persons" or will say they are "good people" they just do not go to Church. "All good works put together are not equivalent to the Sacrifice of the Mass, because they are the works of men and the Holy Mass is the work of God."[10]

There are two questions I would like to address. The three kings, or magi; why did they come? Why did they go? Imagine this: three astrologers traditionally from the continents known to man at that time. There was one representing Africa; another from Asia, and one from Europe. Not Jewish, but pagan Gentile nations. Three astrologers from three different territories coming together in one pursuit.

Granted the Gospel never states how many kings there were, and yet it tells what each king brought with him. Gold...for a king; frankincense, for a God; and myrrh for a human who would one day die. What would drive one to seek Jesus? Ones who knew not the prophecies of Isaiah. But ones who did know something was missing that this world could not provide. Something for which they would surrender their kingdom and those they loved for awhile. And yet another king sought him too.

Herod also sought Jesus, but not to worship. Whenever goodness is born, evil is not satisfied with simply denying it, but seeks to destroy it. And so, when wise men seek Jesus, it is always to worship him or destroy him. How is it, that an infant, put such fear into a king? Or is it possible that even evil believes in the Truth?

But back to the three Magi... why didn't they remain? Once they found all they desired, then why did they leave? Because they had to return to give the gift they themselves had received. They had to come down from the mountain. They who worshiped stars, now worshiped the One who created the stars. The magi didn't go to church either, until they beheld the one that gave them life and breath. They didn't go to church, until they knelt at the manger of

---

10 Jean-Marie Baptiste Vianney, as quoted in John Paul II, *Holy Thursday Letters to My Brother Priests*, Ed. by James P. Socias, (Chicago: Midwest Theological Forum, 1992), 165.

the one who was there from the beginning, and it changed them forever.

The man who approached me at the table, did so because I was a priest. He too, was searching for Christ, because the stars did not satisfy him. He too, was waiting for the epiphany, so that for maybe the first time in his life, he might have a reason to be the person he'd always hoped he could be. And who knows…for the first time that night, he might have received a different kind of Spirit.

The Feast of the Baptism of the Lord

Isaiah 42: 1-4, 6-7; Acts 10: 34-38; Luke 3: 15-16; 21-22; Psalm 29

Here is my servant...my chosen one.

Listen to the words of the Prophet Isaiah: *Thus says the LORD: Here is my servant whom I uphold, my chosen one with whom I am pleased, upon whom I have put my spirit.* Luke echoes these words in his Gospel:...*the skies opened and the Holy Spirit descended on him in visible form like a dove. A voice from heaven was heard to say, "You are my beloved Son. On you my favor rests."*

The vocation of the priest or the religious is not for the sake of the individual called, so much as it is for those he is called to serve. And he is called, not because he is better than those who he is called to serve, but on the contrary, because he is one of those who also needs the Divine Healer. And having experienced such a miracle, he can offer the same miracle to others.

I recall a tragedy that we had at the high school. I was at my hermitage and got the call late one night that a student had died suddenly. Fr. LaVoie was at the scene, as I was en route, and I was grateful for that at least. It was a tragedy...a young life gone, and a devastated family left in the wake. I knew the child, and he was a treasure. The next day at school there would only be freshman and sophomores present, because it was prom weekend and the upperclassmen had the day off. We knew the next day would prove difficult, but I had no idea to what extent.

A number of priests showed up to counsel students, and I don't believe any one of them was without a line at the door all day. We decided to celebrate Mass at the end of the day to mourn the loss of this student. As we prepared, students were scurrying around to choose readings and set up the auditorium, while others were sending text messages (illegally I might add) to the juniors and seniors at home. But the end of the day, we arrived at the auditorium for Mass and I couldn't believe it: Many of the juniors and seniors were there, on a day they didn't have to be, to celebrate Mass for this student. I remained at the school that day with a number of students, while speaking with the parents of the deceased a few times a day.

At the end of the day, I was on my way back from the school and I was told that there was an emergency baptism needed at the Medical Center. I rushed over there to pediatric Intensive Care Unit. It was all I could do to speak to the parents without "losing it". Here was this three-year-old with tubes and wires everywhere. His belly was swollen from infection and there stood his helpless parents. I baptized the child, flubbing through the words, trying to keep my composure. I assured them of my prayers, having taken the information, and then returned to my car in the fire lane outside. I put down my sick call kit with trembling hands and I sobbed. I don't think I cried like that in years, but the flood began. I can't imagine what the people walking by must have thought, as they saw this priest just weeping, and yet in that moment, I felt as helpless as those parents in the room with their child. *He chooses the weak, and makes them strong...*

The same is true for each of us. Saint Peter says: *I begin to see how true it is that God shows no partiality. Rather, the man of any nation who fears God and acts uprightly is acceptable to him.* What Peter says to Cornelius in the Acts of the Apostles is true for each of us. As Catholic Christians, God has chosen each of us for a specific purpose within the kingdom. And just as a priest or religious is not chosen for their own sake, or because they are better than anyone else, we each have been chosen by God, despite our infirmities. For sometimes, it is through our infirmities that we are invited into the world of a soul. Sometimes it is weeping with those who weep and grieving with those who grieve, that we are finally invited into their world.

He painted a sign advertising the twenty pups, and set about nailing it to a post on the edge of his yard. As he was driving the last nail into the post, he felt a tug on his overalls. He looked down into the eyes of a little boy. "Mister," the little one said, "I want to buy one of your puppies." "Well," said the farmer, as he rubbed the sweat off the back of his neck, "These puppies come from fine parents and cost a good deal of money."

The boy dropped his head for a moment. Then reaching deep into his pocket, he pulled out a handful of change and held it up to the farmer. "I've got thirty-nine cents. Is that enough to take a look?" "Sure," said the farmer. And with that he let out a whistle. The little boy pressed his face against the chain-link fence. His eyes danced with delight. As the dogs made their way to the fence, the little boy noticed something else stirring inside the doghouse. Slowly another little ball appeared; this one noticeably smaller. Down the ramp it slid. Then in a somewhat awkward manner, the little pup began hobbling toward the others, doing its best to catch up....

"I want that one," the little boy said, pointing to the runt. The farmer knelt down at the boy's side and said, "Son, you don't want that puppy. He will never be able to run and play with you like these other dogs would."

With that the little boy stepped back from the fence, reached down, and began rolling up one leg of his trousers. In doing so, he revealed a steel brace running down both sides of his leg attaching itself to a specially made shoe. Looking back up at the farmer, he said, "You see sir, I don't run too well myself, and he will need someone who understands."[11]

I called the Medical Center late the next day and said to the nurse on duty: "Is Sam still alive? Did he make it?" She responded that she could not tell me that information. "Well then tell me this…is Sam still a resident there?" I could hear the smile in her voice. "Yes, father, Sam is still a resident here." And my smile joined her own.

---

11 Internet Forward

Sometimes the Lord allows us to be afflicted, and yet this is not a weakness, but a strength. *A bruised reed he shall not break, and a smoldering wick he shall not quench...* "He who is divine became human...so that we who are human, might become divine."[12]

---

12   Saint Athanasius, *On the Incarnation*, 54.

SECOND SUNDAY IN
TEMPUS PER ANNUM

ISAIAH 62: 1-5; 1 CORINTHIANS 12: 4-11;
JOHN 2: 1-12; PSALM 96

Do whatever He tells you…only what He tells you to do.

A few years ago, I was taking a short vacation in New York with three other priests, and we had a wonderful time. At the end of that trip, however, I herniated a disc in my back, and the Doctor said it would take a month or so until things were back to normal.

Although Fr. Helwig and Fr. King were taking good care of me, I decided to recover the weekend at my parents' house. Recovery….well let me tell you…I still haven't recovered from that experience! Just to give you a sample, the first night, my mother came in and began to set up the card table in the bedroom, and when I asked what she was doing she told me: "Me and your daddy are going to eat dinner with you." And that set the tone for the whole three days.

She would say, "Honey, don't you want something else to drink, other than water?" "No mom, thank you." "No? Are you sure? We have iced tea, lemonade, Sprite, Coca Cola.." "No mom, I'm fine." "We have milk, coffee, root beer, are you sure?" "YES! Yes…I'm sure." "How about your pillas? You don't look comfortable, can I get you some more pillas?" "No mom, I have plenty of pillows, I'm comfortable, thank you." "How about for your legs? That doctor said to prop up your legs, don't you want…" "I'm fine! Please! I just need to go to the bathroom." And she walked out. When I came out of the bathroom, there must have been ten pillows on the bed! My back recovered in a few weeks, but I'm still in recovery from that weekend at home. My therapist says I'm making progress!

There were many who said: "Maybe this is God telling you to slow down." I considered that, and then thought...*nahhh*. But there was a message among the many the Lord was giving me over that period of time.

Jesus makes two requests of the people at the wedding. And Mary says: "Do whatever He tells you." The two requests Jesus makes are these: "Fill the jars" and "Take this to the steward." That's it. That wasn't enough for me though...I wanted to turn the water into wine. The Lord reminded me, in a very real way, that my job is to fill the jugs with water; my job is to take the wine to where it needs to go. He'll make the water into wine.

Sin is always an effort to grasp those things we were never meant to have or to do those things we are not called to do. The Lord reminded me that it is not for me to change water into wine...that's His job. Perhaps he also gave another lesson, very subtly, in the time spent with my parents, trapped in their house. All that is necessary is to listen to the voice of the mother...the one who says: "Do whatever He tells you."

THIRD SUNDAY IN
TEMPUS PER ANNUM

NEHEMIAH 8: 2-4, 5-6, 8-10; 1 COR. 12: 12-30; LUKE 1: 1-4, 4:14-21; PSALM 19

Pro-Life and Christian Unity

Our voice in this world is drowning quickly. There are many voices crying out in the wilderness, but the problem is they are not united in their cry. Early in this century, the Christian denominations of this country, although different on dogmatic points, were united on moral issues for the most part. That union began to crumble in the 1930's when certain denominations decided, in an effort not to exclude anyone, to weaken their moral standpoints, and the slippery slope quickly became too steep to remain grounded in anything.

As I watched the news, I saw a story that had to do with a woman and her partner in the company who have made embryos available for any couple who wishes to have one implanted. They have résumés for these embryos, as though they were applying to Harvard. They have the parents' IQ results, transcripts, physical attributes, and they say it's all in an effort to give parents the child they want, as opposed to simply accepting whatever they receive.

Our voice in the world is drowning quickly. These *news people* were giving accolades to this woman and her company for using technology to help people...to help people what? Design their child...without the aid of God. Their voice is the one that is heard. What about our own? This weekend is deemed Christian Unity Sunday. Although there are many Dogmatic issues that separate us from other Christian denominations, we cannot risk the detriment that our division on moral issues presents. We must be united. As this weekend is Christian

Unity weekend, it is also the weekend preceding the "March for Life" in Washington DC. We have a bus leaving tomorrow filled with students who will represent our Church and High School at this march.

The Evangelist Luke Writes: *I too have decided, after investigating everything accurately anew, to write it down in an orderly sequence for you, most excellent Theophilus, so that you may realize the certainty of the teachings you have received.* The Name *Theophilus* means God-Lover. Luke, here, wants to set everyone straight. He doesn't mince words. He wants us to be a united voice, as Paul says: *"One Body" though many parts.* Each part is necessary in order for the body, united to act.

Jesus says, amidst criticism and persecution in the synagogue: *The Spirit of the Lord is upon me, because he has anointed me to bring glad tidings to the poor.* The only acceptable year is one in which we can finally unite our hearts and voices so that we might *out- cry* those who would see the evils in this world persist, because of our division.

In her *Interior Castle*, St. Teresa of Avila writes: "…here the devils once more show the soul these vipers—that is, the things of the world – and they pretend that earthly pleasures are almost eternal."[13] How tragic that lives are being sacrificed as collateral damage to the divisions in the *Body of Christ*. But what if we were united? What if we accepted our calling? Well, then we would be the ones *to bring glad tidings to the poor*…especially the ones who have no voice but our own.

---

13 Saint Theresa of Avila, *Interior Castle*, Translated and Edited by E. Allison Peers, (New York: Doubleday Press, 1989), 48.

FOURTH SUNDAY IN
TEMPUS PER ANNUM

JEREMIAH 1: 4-5, 17-19; 1 COR. 12: 31-13:13; LUKE 4: 21-30; PSALM 71

"Love never fails…"

We can't believe it! It can't possibly be true. That such a thing that is "selfless" exists. We can't believe that something as perfect and powerful and omniscient as God, loved us into existence. We can't believe that someone could've created the world without us in it… but He didn't. We are unwilling to believe someone who knew us even before He *formed us in the womb* could *appoint us a prophet to the nations;* could *make us a fortified city;* and *will be with [us] to deliver [us].* One who loves us as though we were the only creature.

If this is true, why would anyone; how could anyone ever deny the Creator? If sin is the denial of God, then we have no need to judge harshly and condemn the sinner, because without God their very life will be torture enough, and the emptiness they live, a taste of hell. Can there be a problem that is even similar in magnitude to denial of God and not offering *Him* our love? I think one of the greatest poverties we experience is not allowing God, to love us.

What do we mean by love? What does Paul mean? Paul lays it out in very straight-forward terms: If you are a CEO; if you are a great artist; if you are a wonderful musician; if you are brilliant in all the most difficult subjects in the world; if you speak several languages; if you are the MVP on your team; if you are the strongest person in the world; even if your faith in God is tried and true…but you have not love…it is all worthless! What *is* this love?

In the ancient world, there were four words commonly used in Greek for love. I would like to bring to mind three of the four that were used. The first was *philios*. *Philios* was used to describe a "friendship" type of love. The name "Phila delphia" comes from *philios* and *adelphos* (brother) thus "the city of brotherly love." The second word was *eros*. *Eros* is more of a romantic love between spouses or lovers. We get the word "erotic" from that word. These two words have in common the fact that they are a love for something because it is desirable. The third word is different. The third word, *agape*, is an unconditional love; a love for something, even though it is undesirable. This love, is the love of the Creator. This is the love, we are called to offer, being in His *image* and *likeness*.

Two of my nephews, Krystopher and Mason, were wild when they were four and six years old. But when I went to their house to get them wound up and then leave them to my sister, and her husband (just kidding, I would never do that...no I'm not) I rang the doorbell a certain way every time. As I waited, I would hear the stampede thumping across the floor screaming wildly. As I would enter the room, they would jump on me, and I'd tickle them and give them "flirbirts[14]", as they laughed and carried on.

We were one-on-one, just simply enjoying life. There were no expectations except to "play with us!" They gave me a kiss and said, "I love you untle Mite". THAT WAS IT! Think about your own kids; or if you don't have kids, others' children. That was the love fully expressed without doubt or insecurity or inhibitions...a true love. Listen to the psalmist: *For you are my hope, O Lord; my trust, O God, from my youth. On you I depend from my birth; from my mother's womb you are my strength.* I imagine that is what God remembers too. He remembers a time when we were so easy to love, and He relished our openness and our need for Him. "We all need more love than we deserve."[15] The great sin of the people in the gospel, was that they were

---

14 **Flirbirt:** When one places one's mouth on the belly of a baby and blows, making an obscene sound which normally will cause said infant to laugh out loud.
15 Fr. Peter Van Breeman. *The God Who Won't Let Go*, (Notre Dame, IN: Ave Maria Press, 2001), 21.

refusing God's love; God's gift. *God so loved the world that He gave us His only son…*

Just as kids do, however, I imagine my nephews will grow up. We begin to doubt it is possible for anyone to love us so much, unconditionally, even when we sin. Because of this, we refuse to allow the love of God to touch us. And so just as the people in the Gospel, we will be unable to experience any miracle. Perhaps if we just listened to the prescription Jesus offers again and again, perhaps for the first time in our life, we might experience the miracle; we might appreciate the *agape* love our Father has for us. *You must become like little children. He who does not become like a little child, will never enter the kingdom of God.*

FIFTH SUNDAY IN
TEMPUS PER ANNUM

ISAIAH 6: 1-2, 3-8; 1 CORINTHIANS 15: 1-11;
LUKE 5: 1-11; PSALM 138

Whom shall I send?[16]

Disciples. We hear throughout the scriptures, but especially in the New Testament, about the "disciples." Sometimes, it appears that the words apostles and disciples, are used interchangeably, but that is not necessarily true. Apostle comes from the Greek, *apostallos*, which means "one who is sent." Disciple comes from the Latin word *discipulus*, which means "student." There were twelve disciples, then there were seventy-two disciples, and then some left. The number of Apostles seems to be stable at twelve; whereas, the disciples were many and varied. So what was a disciple?

When we consider that disciple means "student," then we must assume a teacher was involved. Without a teacher, we really can't be a disciple. But then, teachers were not *always* teachers, so they must have been students at some point as well. Therefore, these teachers were at one time the disciple. Do we ever stop learning? If the answer is no, then the fact is that many *teachers* are also *disciples*. So…if all of this makes sense, then all we do as *disciples* is pass on what we are given. Does this make sense? Okay…let's see if I can mess this up now.

Seated behind me is the man who taught me much of what I know about Scripture. He is one of many scholars who have dedicated their lives to the study of Sacred Scripture. He is my teacher. You

---

16 This homily was given at St. Louis de Marillac in the presence of my Scripture professor from St. Vincent Seminary, Fr. Patrick Cronauer, OSB.

think *you're* intimidated at times? Imagine preaching on the subject at Mass, with your teacher behind you. It's like a holy comprehensive exam with the proctor seated in the celebrant's chair. Welcome to my world! (I'm standing here, interpreting Isaiah) "What Isaiah meant was *this"* (and then I turn around and face Fr. Patrick)… "right?" And then I begin to expound again, "And the people at that time felt like this" (again I turn and face him)… "didn't they?"

I mention Fr. Patrick because I can see the Gospel very much alive in him. I imagine at times, our class of men frustrated him, or made him doubt…*not me of course, but you know…the rest of the class.* And I also imagine that like Peter in the Gospel, Fr. Patrick would say at times: "Master I've worked at it all day and night and they just aren't getting it," and Jesus beckons, "Put down deep, and do it again". Thank God he did, because sure enough, he was faithful and obedient, and I'm a priest today! Paul says: *By God's favor I am what I am.*

Fr. Patrick obviously knows the secret to discipleship. Just as Paul states so eloquently, nothing we have is our own. He writes: *I handed on to you what I also received; the least of the apostles.* Isaiah is the same. He sees himself as unworthy, and then God cleanses his lips and helps him to realize what we should all realize as disciples: *It is not YOU who are speaking…it is I who use you!* Lest we fall into the deadly sin of pride and believe we do these things ourselves, we trust that God will give us what we need, and we attribute all the good we do to Him. The psalmist proclaims: *In the sight of the angels I will praise you Lord..When I called you answered me; you built up strength within me; all the kings of the earth shall give thanks to you O Lord.*

We are disciples…we are stewards, not owners of the great gifts we have received from our God. We are the students, but we are called also to be the teachers. Fear might seize us, much as it did Isaiah, *Woe is me, I am doomed! For I am a man of unclean lips, living among a people of unclean lips.* And yet, if like Isaiah, we accept the call that each of us has by the very fact that we were created, when God could have chosen not to create us at all; He will give us everything we need. We will come to discover that what began with our creation, will continue with our discipleship, and find its completion in our instruction of others. In the words of the psalmist, *The Lord will complete what He has done for me; in the sight of the angels I will sing your praises Lord.* To serve..."to serve means to bring man to the very foundations of his humanity, to the deepest essence of his dignity."[17]

---

17 John Paul II, *Holy Thursday Letters To My Brother Priests*, Edited by James P. Socias, (Chicago: Midwest Theological Forum, 1992), 136.

SIXTH SUNDAY IN
TEMPUS PER ANNUM

JEREMIAH 17: 5-8; 1 CORINTHIANS 15: 12, 16-20; LUKE 6: 17, 20-26; PSALM 1

The Be-Attitudes[18]

It would appear to me that most people do not positively decide, "I want my mediocrity; I don't want to get better." T. A. Sparks writes: "Spirituality is not a life of suppression. That is negative. Spirituality is positive; it is a new and extra life, not the old one striving to get the mastery of itself."[19] "If you keep doing what you have always been doing, you will keep getting what you have always been getting."[20] It is when we want to make a change that there is positive proof that the Holy Spirit is at work in us.

How does the Holy Spirit work within us? We might have tried many different types of self-help, or even psychiatry. And for some things, that is the way to go; but what so often happens, is we write off the "invisible" for those things we can see. Listen to the prophet Jeremiah: *Cursed is the one who trusts in humans, who seeks his strength in the flesh, whose heart turns away from the Lord.*

Take away the source, and the creature perishes. C.S. Lewis states in his letters:

---

18 I heard this title in a homily offered by Msgr. William Richardson. I took the title, because it was "catchy" and then added my own "take on it." Thank you Bill.
19 T. A. Sparks, in Charles Allen Kollar, *Solution-Focused Pastoral Counseling: An Effective Short-Term Approach for Getting People Back on Track*, (Grand Rapids, MI: Zondervan, 1997), 53.
20 Ibid., 15.

"Keep clear of psychiatrists unless you know they are also close to God. Otherwise they start with the assumption that your religion is an illusion and try to 'cure' it: and this assumption they make not as professional psychologists, but as amateur philosophers."[21]

Jesus gives us some hint in the Gospel today how the Spirit works to draw us closer to God. He offers us four prescriptions for happiness, and four warnings when we're not where we need to be. These prescriptions can often be a bit cloudy, so I hope to put them into the proper context and make them a little more doable. WE will call them the BE-ATTITUDES.

Blessed are the poor. **Be concerned and determined.** One of the traits of mediocre people is that they are at home with their "illness." People who are not worried about what they will eat tomorrow; where they will be; what they will do, can be quite comfortable, without need for the source. Not so with the poor. If we are concerned about where we are, and where we are headed, we will make constant efforts to correct it. If we are concerned, then we will be determined, and the Holy Spirit will work with that determination to bless us with the Kingdom.

Blessed are the hungry. **Be motivated and committed.** Boredom and joy are incompatible. Jesus does not say, "blessed is the one who is hungry." The "YOU" he uses is plural. Our relationship with God is not an exclusive relationship. We are motivated and committed to our faith when we can share it. There is a connection between the beauty of holiness and the fruitfulness of our work and interpersonal relationships. Even if we have a message, if the hearer finds the messenger repulsive, or fake, the message hasn't a hope…it arrives discolored by smelling of the one who uttered it. There is no substitute for authenticity. This requires our commitment… that we are hungry for more, never being satisfied.

Blessed are you who weep, you will laugh. **Be Humble.** Realizing that what we have is total gift. We have done nothing to be given such gifts,

---

21 C. S. Lewis, *Letters of C.S. Lewis*, Ed. By W. H. Lewis, (London: Geoffrey Bles., 1966).

and they could fail or be taken at any time…all is grace. Humility is a prayer that if uttered is always answered. I remember being in college and going over to exercise. I was on the treadmill and there were two girls, one on either side of me, so I pushed it up a notch, and was more or less going at a fast run. Then a girl I knew from chem-lab, who I had been trying to get up the courage to talk to, came through the gym. She glanced my way looked over with a smile very nonchalantly and said: "Hi Mike," and as I looked up, gawking, all I remember is flying in reverse at twenty knots, and the inelastic collision of the gym wall with my back. And then of course, the two girls who were running beside me, picking me up and asking if I was alright. Humility. Weep, I did. But I laugh today, right? Not really.

Finally, *blessed are you when people hate you; exclude and insult you; denounce your name as evil on account of me.* **Be** *persevering.* We are usually pretty good about New Year's resolutions; about Lenten penance in the first week, but after that we realize why it is a resolution or re-solution and penance. How often we hear of finding people who were wrecked or lost, and it happens that when they died, they were only yards away from help or civilization. If we can see the light, we can survive most anything. Nietzsche states: "He who has a *why* to live for, can endure almost any how."[22] If we can be concerned and determined; if we can be motivated and committed; if we can be humble, then the light will be bright within us.

This is not work of ours, but that of the Holy Spirit. What it is, is an Attitude that enables the Spirit to enter into us. This entrance of the Spirit then empowers us to persevere. If we have a life that

---

22 Frederick Nietsche, in Viktor Fankl, *Man's Search for Meaning*, (New York: Simon and Schuster, 1984), 109. I need to note here that Nietzsche denied God all his life, and yet if we read his letters, we see in them a soul yearning for something more. He writes to his sister: "A man of spiritual depth needs friends, unless he still has God as a friend. But I have neither God nor friends." Later he writes this poem: "I want to know You, Unknown One; You who are reaching deep into my soul; And ravaging my life, a savage gale. You Inconceivable yet Related One! I want to know You – even serve." Finally at the age of forty-three he wrote: "I have now lived for forty-three years, and I am just as lonely as I was in the years of my childhood. I wish this man had not read my books. He is too good. My influence on him could be disastrous."

enables the spirit to enter, then often we will be hated, insulted and denounced, because we will remind others of how inadequate they are in their spiritual life. Jesus always spoke the truth with conviction and compassion, but he always spoke the truth. He was loved by many, because he introduced them to possibility; and hated by others, because he reminded them of their inadequacy.

Jesus then offers the woes. A woe is not so much a curse as a warning to all of those who do not have the Spirit and will not create a disposition open to the Spirit. They will forever be empty, because we, who were not made for this world, can never be satisfied by the things of this world. Only the Breath, who was breathed into us from the beginning, is the one who can fill us, if we have but one thing. *BE-ATTITUDE.*

Ash Wednesday
(See Appendix V, Number -3-)

First Sunday of Lent

Deuteronomy 26: 4-10; Romans 10: 8-13;
Luke 4: 1-13 Psalm 91

If you are the Son of God, turn these stones into bread. We need not go further than that. What would be wrong with turning stones into bread? Absolutely nothing...unless you are God. Jesus never performed a miracle for himself. Whereas we have this tendency within to want to *self*-preserve, or *self*-serve, he had a tendency to consider the other.

Jesus is "led" into the desert by the Spirit (the Greek word used, *ekballō*, actually means "thrown out") and there, he will experience the Exodus. Make no mistake, the Messiah will lead the Israelites through a new Exodus. The difference is that not all will accompany him. He passes through the desert and is offered the same temptations the Israelite people will be offered. The evil one preys on Jesus' hunger; preys on his power; and preys on a "promised land."

He heard our cry and saw our affliction, our toil and our oppression. He brought us out of Egypt with his strong hand and outstretched arm, with terrifying power, with signs and wonders. In this statement is Jesus' strength. Jesus knows, it is not him, but the One who sent him, from Whom he receives everything. And because of that, he will not fall into the trap that Moses himself fell into; he will not fall into the trap of believing he should be worshiped or should not suffer. And because of this, he will be more than a Messiah... he will be God.

So the desert of Lent should hold no fear for us, unless we treat it as just another part of the Church year; unless we treat it as the rest of the days. If it does not create pause, or "lead" us to reflect, then we should be afraid. Because we will not put the blood on our doorposts, we will not be ready for flight; we will miss the Passover, and therefore, will never realize the freedom of our Exodus.

Second Sunday of Lent

Genesis 15: 5-12, 17-18; Philippians 3: 17-4:1; Luke 9: 28-36 Psalm 27

Promise and fulfillment.

All of our sacred deposit of faith…all of our Theology and Scripture…the Tradition that leads us from day to day…all of it, is based on the fulfillment of a promise. I know it's difficult to understand "promise" in a world that does not see the power of a promise…in a world that does not keep its promises.

Scott Hahn in his book, *The Father who Keeps His Promises*, begins with a great story of such a promise.

> …Over thirty thousand were dead from a magnitude 8.2 earthquake that rocked and nearly flattened Armenia in 1989. In the muddled chaos, a distressed father bolted through the winding streets leading to the school where his son had gone earlier that morning. The man couldn't stop thinking about the promise he'd given his son many times: "No matter what happens, Armand, I'll always be there."

> He reached the site where the school had been but saw only a pile of rubble. He just stood there at first, fighting back the tears, and then took off, stumbling over debris, toward the east corner where he knew his son's classroom had been. With nothing but his bare hands, he started to dig. He was desperately pulling up bricks and pieces of wall-plaster, while others stood by watching in forlorn disbelief. He heard someone growl, "Forget it, mister. They're all dead." He looked up, flustered, and replied, "You can grumble, or you can help me lift these bricks."

He kept digging and digging – for hours...twelve hours... eighteen hours...twenty-four hours...thirty-six hours...Finally, into the thirty-eighth hour, he heard a muffled groan from under a piece of wallboard. He seized the board, pulled it back and cried, "Armand!" From the darkness came a slight shaking voice, "Papa...!?" Other weak voices began calling out, as the young survivors stirred beneath the still uncleared rubble. Gasps and shouts of bewildered relief came from the few onlookers and parents who remained. They found fourteen of the thirty-three students still alive. When Armand finally emerged, he tried to help dig, until all his surviving classmates were out.

Everybody standing there heard him as he turned to his friends and said, "See, I told you my father wouldn't forget us."[23]

The *Promise* begins with creation, and continues with re-creation. In the Ancient Near East of Abraham's time, one of the most important cultural pressures was to have children (quite opposite from our current culture, in this country at least). This is why God's promise rings so loudly in the ears of Abraham: *Look up at the sky and count the stars, if you can. Just so, shall your descendants be. I am the Lord who brought you from Ur of the Chaldeans to give you this land as a possession.* The God who created the universe; who controls life and death, health and sickness, can certainly deliver on promises.

We have our citizenship in heaven; it is from there that we eagerly await the coming of our Savior, the Lord Jesus Christ. The promises God makes in this world, will secure our presence in the next, but every promise is a gift...and what is necessary is for the other to receive the gift. To receive a promise, necessitates faith in the one who offers it. The opposite of a promise, is a lie. This is why Satan is the "father of lies." The only reason anyone will lie, is that they lack power. The God who makes promises has all power, because if He dislikes something, He need only change it. This is our God...the Father who keeps His promises.

---

23 Scott Hahn, *A Father Who Keeps His Promises: God's Covenant Love in Scripture,* (Ann Arbor Michigan: Servant Publications, 1998), 13-14.

Just as the son in the story, we too await in the rubble of this world, for the Father to rescue us. We wait amidst the disasters and quakes; the plague and sickness for a Father who will not abandon His own. But He will not force our adoption. We must accept the promise and the responsibilities that come with such a promise. That as He draws us from the rubble of our sin, He might say: "There now…my beloved…my chosen one…with whom I am well pleased.

Third Sunday of Lent

Exodus 3:1-8, 13-15; 1 Corinthians 10: 1-6, 10-12; Luke 13: 1-9 Psalm 103

Hope is often the fruit of crisis.

I think you would agree with me when I say that one of the worst feelings we can experience as humans, is hopelessness. It is a feeling of being out of control, with no good alternatives in sight. A feeling of solitude; of being trapped or stuck; of being utterly alone. How can someone move forward in their spiritual life, let alone their emotional and physical life, when they are so stuck in this hopelessness?

Reading about Moses gives me some consolation. He's in the desert with his father-in-law's sheep... but why? Because he's on the run! He's a wanted man, on charges of murdering an Egyptian. His life is essentially over. He can never go home again, and he's pretty much resigned to the fact that this is what he will be doing for the rest of his life. And then...a burning bush, out in the desert. He had two choices: he could check it out, or walk away. The one choice would change, not only his life forever, but the lives of millions...US! It would change our lives forever.

Don't get me wrong, Moses did go and check it out, but he wasn't committed right away. He could still choose to walk away. Even when he brought the Israelites out of Egypt, he still was unsure. I don't think his lack of faith was in God, so much as it was a lack of faith in himself. He had every excuse for not being the prophet and leader God chose him to be and yet...in the end... he responds: "Here am I Lord." And life has never been the same since.

Saul is a killer of Christians, and is actively persecuting Christ. I imagine, though, that he was also probably searching...trying to figure out why these people were willing to die for a man who was no more than a *faith healer*. He's mulling it over and thinking about Stephen, the first martyr. He thought about how this man who was dying, could forgive his killers, as the "faith healer" had done. As he made his journey toward Damascus, he looked up to heaven and said, "Adonai...show me the way..." and BOOM! He's knocked off his feet. His journey would continue, amidst shipwrecks; imprisonment; persecutions, and he would change a world that did not know Christ.

Isn't it interesting that each of these roadblocks, these impasses in the lives of these two individuals, become doors through which God chose to enter. That perhaps He waits until all the people and things we have counted on for so long are ripped from under our feet, so that as we land prostrate on the dust, we might, for the first time, reach beyond what this world can provide. Perhaps it is in those moments, that for the first time, we might look to Him and like Paul and Moses before him, be changed forever. Cardinal Ratzinger says:

> Being a Christian is essentially conversion, and conversion in the Christian sense is not the changing of a few ideas, but rather a process of death. The limits of the I are broken. The I loses itself in order to find itself anew in a larger subject that spans heaven and earth, past, present, and future, and therein touches truth itself.[24]

God would bring us back from the dead through his ultimate sacrifice...His very life; but *not without our desire*. The gospel speaks of this master who is impatient with the fruitfulness of a tree. This Master is intolerant and will not wait for change. He has no investment other than the fruit. The parable Jesus tells of the fig tree is a wonderful illustration of possibility. A fig tree normally takes about three years to bear fruit. If it doesn't bear fruit by that time, it probably never will bear any at all. The parable does not speak to a landowner who will allow the tree to reap the benefits without the cost. In the same respect, there is opportunity on two fronts. The gardener, has planted the seed; has nurtured the plant and watched it from the beginning. From that fact alone, He wants to give the plant a second chance. He

---

24 Joseph Cardinal Ratzinger, *Images of Hope: Meditations on Major Feasts*, (San Francisco: Ignatius Press, 2006), 71.

is willing to work harder; put his reputation on the line, just to give a second chance.

This is our God. Paul says: *These things happened as examples for us, so that we might not desire evil things, as they did. Do not grumble as some of them did, and suffered death by the destroyer.* We can give the plant the proper nutrients; soil; water; we can even talk to the plant, and it may still die. (I have witnessed many plants dying at my hands, and I am a biologist!) It is up to the plant to grow.

The fact is, we can go through life, floundering as we go from one fad to another; seeing one guru or another therapist to get us unstuck, only to flounder again…or we can trust. We can use our roadblock in life as an opportunity to grow toward the One who planted the seed from the beginning, and every day waits patiently for the fruit that will come, when we allow it. And manure…manure's a funny thing. Manure by itself, stinks; but placed properly with nourishment and water, it grows a strong plant that bears much fruit; if…we can put up with the stink.

Listen to the psalmist and see if this isn't the divine Gardner at work: *The Lord is kind and merciful; He pardons all your iniquities, he heals all your ills. He redeems your life from destruction, he crowns you with kindness and compassion.* Does that sound like hopelessness? The message is simple: For those who have faith; for those who can patiently wait for the gardener and use the suffering they have experienced to reach beyond themselves, hope never fails.

Lent is this time. If you are at a moment in your life where suffering is your bread; if you are feeling stuck; if you're confused or unsure where to go, Lent is the perfect time to reach beyond yourself. One of the worst days in human history was Good Friday, and the suffering of the Christ. One of the best days in human history was Good Friday, where suffering became for us, salvation. "There will come a time when you believe that everything is finished…that will be the beginning."[25]

---

25 Louis L'Amour, *Lonely on the Mountain*, (New York: Bantam Books).

FOURTH SUNDAY OF LENT

JOSHUA 5: 9, 10-12; 2 CORINTHIANS 5: 17-21; LUKE 15: 1-3, 11-32 PSALM 34

The God of second chance

I imagine many people are afraid of the Sacrament of Reconciliation; or perhaps they don't see the point of the whole thing. Many have preconceived ideas which are wrong regarding the sacrament. This is evidenced by empty confessionals; scores of people coming to communion, but not confessing. Why? What is the sacrament of Reconciliation?

I imagine that at some point in your life, you have experienced a death. I would say we've all lost someone in our life who meant a great deal to us. Remember what that was like? Perhaps, it is still very vivid, because it was not long ago, or because it has taken so long to heal from that loss. You remember the feelings. The painful numbness that you felt. A pain that you couldn't point to in a physical way, because it was enmeshed within your whole being. Lewis describes it like this:

> No one ever told me that grief felt so like fear. I am not afraid, but the sensation is like being afraid. The same fluttering in the stomach, the same restlessness, the yawning. I keep on swallowing...I want others to be around me. I dread the moments when the house is empty. If only they would talk to one another and not to me.[26]

The rawness of it, knowing that a part of you has gone. The feeling of being deserted, and left alone...completely alone. We remember these feelings because they are so painful; because they take their toll on us.

---

26 C. S. Lewis, *A Grief Observed*, (New York: Bantam Books, 1976), 1-2.

I imagine this is what God feels like every time we sin. Whenever we purposely turn away from God, He experiences this "death of His loved one" again and again. "No sin can touch one of God's stars or silence one of His words, but it can cruelly wound His Heart."[27] Can you imagine the magnitude. We may experience this pain with one... God experiences this pain millions of times each minute...but it is different. Imagine if you could bring your loved one back from the dead. What sacrifices would we be willing to make to do this? Yet it is impossible on the one hand, and on the other, would they even want to come back? Yet for God...this *is* possible. What would He do, in order to bring one back from the dead? Make the ultimate sacrifice.

And yet, we know we will fail...we choose against God, and so have died to Him. But our Lord, merciful and patient, has given us a means by which to put forth fruit. He has given us the means to come back to life again, we need only be open to it. There are some things God will not do. He will not forgive a heart that is closed to forgiveness. Our relationship with God is like a rope. We are anchored....we are connected. When we sin, we turn away, we sever this rope. We are no longer anchored...we have gone away from God, and He grieves that loss. But if we turn back; if we desire to be raised, He reaches out, and pulls us close, tying a knot in the rope. And as any rope that is cut, once tied again it is not as long as it once was...it is shorter and so we are drawn closer to God. If we remain dead...unanchored, we will be separated from God. And if enough time passes, there is a void through which we can no longer see him.

Remember the grief you felt with the death of your loved one. Imagine the grief caused by thousands of deaths...and imagine that through a singular privilege offered by a God who would rather sacrifice and die Himself than be separated from the creatures, we have an opportunity at a second chance. This...is the sacrament of Reconciliation.

---

27 Bishop Fulton Sheen, *The Priest is not His Own*, (New York: McGraw-Hill, 1963), 155.

Fifth Sunday of Lent

Isaiah 43: 16-21; Philippians 3: 8-14; John 8: 1-11
Psalm 126

"Then he looked up at her..."and offered her a miracle!

Barrels and barrels of ink have been spilled over this Gospel passage in John. The "Woman caught in Adultery" was purported to have been Mary Magdalene, and yet in none of the Gospels, or any other New Testament document does it ever say Mary Magdalene was an adulteress or prostitute. The only place in scripture, that has anything to say about her former life, is the Gospel of Mark where it states she was the woman *from whom Jesus cast out seven demons.*

In any case, if we get too caught up in the details and the "who's who," we might miss the meaning that the evangelist hopes to bring forth through this miracle...it *was* a miracle you know. Picture this just for a moment, and hopefully you will discover why this encounter with Christ was so miraculous.

Here is a woman caught in adultery, which implied three things: there was another person involved, who we hear nothing about. This was probably a man, and so the likelihood he would be charged with anything, is slim to none. Secondly, they must have been watching her in order to catch her in the sin, which places on them a certain degree of sin. Finally, if the woman was caught in the act, she was either half naked or completely naked at the time she is apprehended. Now, take just a moment and reflect on the scene.

Here is a woman, caught in the act of adultery, and dragged through town. A "parade" of sorts would ensue, in that the friends and neighbors, children and adults would line the streets to see the spectacle, which was this naked woman being tossed through town.

People would be shouting obscenities and throwing things at her; they would be laughing, all of them, children and adults; young and old. And finally, having survived the taunts and scorn of people this girl may have known all her life, she is discarded at the feet of the one she has probably wanted to meet for several weeks, months, maybe years. The one she thought, "If I can only touch the hem of the garment, my life will change forever." She wanted to meet this one they said could be the *Messiah*; but not like this. Picture the scene; and that is all in the first two verses of the Gospel passage. Now, the miracle.

They bring her to the feet of Jesus, right as he is teaching. How ironic, because this will be a teachable moment for all. As they approach, they raise the accusation, quoting scripture to him, not unlike the manner in which he was quoted scripture in the desert. This woman should die, according to the Law. Jesus, squatting on the ground, begins to trace with his finger in the dust and probably said something like this: "You're right. According to the law, she deserves death. So go ahead, stone her. Which one should start the stoning you ask? The one who has not sinned, of course! Whichever one of you has never accused anyone falsely; whichever one of you are not looking on this woman in lust right now; whichever one of you did not enjoy watching her in the sinful act. That one of you who is sinless; *you* may stone her." And then he began to trace in the dust again. He looked up and asked her where her persecutors had gone. And since she had none, he said, neither would he persecute her. She was to go…and not sin again.

Now…what was it he wrote in the dust? I mean think about it: this is the only story in all of the New Testament, where it says that Jesus wrote something. What did he write? Some say the names of the sinners in the group, while others say he wrote their sins, and yet not a soul recorded what Jesus actually wrote. Are you kidding me!? The Son of God writes something in the dust, and no one thought it was important enough to record what it was that he wrote? Unless…unless what he wrote, wasn't nearly as important as *why* he wrote.

Think about this. The woman was dragged through town, naked; she was mocked and spit upon; curses and slanders were cast her way and she is tossed at the feet of the man who many say could be the Son of God. What would she have looked like? Where would her eyes have been? Jesus writes in the soil and when he looks up at her, speaks to her. He looks right into her eyes and forgives her sin. *That,* is the miracle. You see, this woman was dead...she had a death sentence placed on her head, and Jesus gave her that second chance. But what's more, the reason Jesus wrote in the dust, was so that he would be, where her eyes were. He squatted down to write in the dust, so that when he looked up at her, he would be looking into the windows of the soul.

Doubt this for a minute? Listen to Isaiah, His prophet: *Remember not the events of the past, the things of long ago consider not; See, I am doing something new! Now it springs forth, do you not perceive it? In the desert I make a way, in the wasteland, rivers.* Our God is such that, again and again, He will squat down into the dust, just to look into the eyes of the sinner... and offer new life. And that...that is truly a miracle!

Passion Sunday of Lent

Gospel for Procession with Palms:
Luke 19: 28-40

Isaiah 50: 4-7; Philippians 2: 6-11;
Luke 22: 14-23:56 Psalm 22

Fulton Sheen would say: "There are two ways of knowing how good God is: one is by never losing Him, and the other is by losing Him and finding Him again."[28] Somehow it seems most often that those who are most dedicated to God, are so dedicated because they went through a time in their life without Him; and having found Him again, rejoice every single day. We don't often talk about sin, and the ugliness of sin. We don't often want to focus on how the things we do, really do affect those around us, whether we believe it or not.

"The more one loves, the more one shrinks from hurting the beloved, and the more one grieves at having done so."[29] True love for the beloved is demonstrated when we act in the best interest of the other. We do not do it out of fear, or concern for disobeying a law, so much as we do it out of our desire to please the other. What is important is to look at how we are living now, and notice how different it is from the people we hear about today. Is it plausible that we who sing "Hosanna in the highest," as we do if we attend Mass on Sunday every week, can also shout "Crucify Him!" as we leave the parking lot to begin our week. It was not only Jesus who quoted the Psalm from today, "why have you forsaken me?" but these words can also be found on the lips of our God, whom we should love above all things, when He sees how far we've strayed.

---

28 Bishop Fulton Sheen, *Peace of Soul*, (New York: McGraw-Hill, 1949), 201.
29 Ibid., 202.

Holy Thursday

(See Appendix I)

Good Friday

(See Appendix II)

EASTER (CYCLE ABC)
EASTER SUNDAY

ACTS 10: 34, 37-43; COLOSSIANS 3: 1-4; JOHN 20: 1-9
PSALM 118

Today we celebrate the highest point in the Church year. But I would be remiss if I didn't recount what has occurred in the days preceding this one. It would be like reading the final chapter, without knowing what the rest of the book was about.

On Holy Thursday, we commemorated our reception of the greatest gift the Lord has given us....Himself. He gave the Eucharist to all of his disciples, and then washed their feet, even knowing that one would betray him, one would deny him and the rest would desert him. From there we followed him into the garden which would begin his passion on Good Friday. Having been deserted by those he loved, he begins his journey in solitude. Smitten and scourged for our offenses. And yet as he takes his last breath breathing forgiveness he gasps: "It is finished." He rejected all temptation and overcame the evil one, perfectly and completely, dying between two thieves.

This should not surprise us, but would foreshadow that his Church would always be persecuted and crucified among thieves. But this is not the end. The Jewish Sabbath was Friday evening and Saturday. And so we celebrate that after three days in the tomb, over which the last day was the Jewish Sabbath, on the eighth day, Sunday, He IS RISEN!

THIS IS OUR FAITH!

But do not let your hearts be troubled. Mary approaches the tomb with the other Mary on the *eighth day*. As the angel approaches, the guards are as dead men. Isn't it ironic that those who were living, appeared as dead, and the one who was to be dead WAS NOW ALIVE! And as Mary approaches, she will experience déjà vous. For the phrase the angel voiced to a young virgin at the beginning of her journey into motherhood, he would now repeat at the end of her journey as a childless widow, "Do not be afraid." He then says to them *You seek the dead among the living.* We cannot afford to make that same mistake. If we do, then we are worse off than those who don't believe at all. WE become the atheists who attend Church, and the Gospel becomes no more than myths and stories that children may read. We need something to hold onto. THIS IS OUR FAITH! Something that in the midst of solitude and isolation, we feel connected, we feel alive. That even through the darkness our hand is grasped by another.

Why would anyone not want something so great? Why would anyone ever stay away from something that is so life-giving; so enlivening; so REAL? Why? I speak to those who have just been brought into the Church recently; to those who have remained here for years, having not run away even when tempted to; to those who have come back after years of being away; to those who are passing through. "Welcome Home." We are all a part of each other whether we like it or not….so we might as well like it.

And so we have an obligation to go out of our way, to support those who in isolation or solitude or pain; those who might feel inclined to go away from the Church; to run away from the family. And today, and all through the year, we are given these signs and symbols; we are given days like this one where we feel so at one with one another, and so much a part of something greater than ourselves that we can hold on through those tough times. That is the *Kerygma* that calls us home again and again…if we can simply embrace the suffering of Christ, then we can also experience the resurrection.

Be not afraid. Jesus is risen as he said. And if this is true, then everything else he said and did is also fulfilled. *Do not let your hearts be troubled. The Father wishes that I should not lose any of whom He gave me. But that I will raise them up on the last day.* To those who have been away… and you know them…tell them someone who loves them is waiting…come home.

DIVINE MERCY SUNDAY
THE SECOND SUNDAY OF EASTER

ACTS 5: 12-16; REVELATION 1: 9-11, 12-13, 17-19; JOHN 20: 19-31 PSALM 118

Peace be with You, Peace be with You, Peace be with You.

Peace be with you! Peace be with you! Peace be with you! Three times throughout this Gospel our Lord will offer those, shut into the upper room, peace. Why three? There seem to be two reasons. First, in Hebrew and Aramaic (the languages which Jesus spoke) there was no superlative degree. We say "I run fast"; "you run faster"; "she runs fastest." But in Hebrew when they want to say "faster" they say "fast, fast". In order to say "fastest" they say, "fast, fast, fast." That's why at Mass we say: "Holy, Holy, Holy Lord." Saying something three times is the best. Jesus wants to give them the fullness of peace.

But I think there was also another reason. The first time he said it, wouldn't register; even the second time was dubitable. Think about it... on the night your Savior needed you most, you denied him; betrayed him; ran away. He told you to wait for him in Galilee, you flee to Emmaus. He told you he would rise again, and you're all holed up in a room because your Messiah is dead. The obvious sentiment of the apostles when the Lord returned was: "Oh crap! He's gonna be mad." After the first "Peace be with you" they were probably thinking... "okay here it comes....remember what he did to that fig tree? Get ready boys." NO no no. (Notice the three times!)

He wanted us to experience the full meaning of the resurrection. The apostles were still experiencing the crucifixion. But alas...one was missing. "One who misses an encounter with the Lord, misses much...

If the minutes of the first Post-resurrection meeting were written down, they would have contained the tragic words of the Gospel: 'Thomas was not there.'"[30] And yet "the doubt of Thomas has done more for the faith of the Church than the belief of all of the other apostles."[31] He was the last to believe, but the first to make a full confession of the Divinity of Christ. *Blessed are those who do not see and yet believe…* that's US! We are the ones who are blessed. So what was the purpose of this first meeting?

Jesus *breathes* his *Spirit* on them. This word in Greek is used in this way nowhere else in the New Testament. The only other place it is found, is the Septuagint (Greek translation of the original Hebrew scriptures). It is found in the book of Genesis, when God *breathes* into the nostrils of the man, Adam. Here, Jesus *breathes* new life into creatures that had no hope of life. Dying, he destroyed our death, but rising, he restored our life.

This is the miracle of Easter. That a Re-Creation has taken place, but only though the sacrifice of the Creator for the Creature. With this *breath*, he gave men the power to forgive sins, or retain them. Why would he ever give this power to men? Because, so much like Thomas and the other Apostles, who believed because they saw, we could offer our sins to God and ask for forgiveness; and yet we would still need so much to see in order to believe; to hear the voice that says, "You are forgiven."

Jesus knew this. He knew that each of his miracles began with a forgiveness of sins, and that it was that freedom from sin which enabled the healing to begin. He knew we would need a human face for the forgiveness that was so generously offered. He knew that in our tendency toward self loathing at times, and insecurity, that we would need one, much like himself, to say: "Peace be with you." "Your sins are forgiven." That we would need someone not only to mend our relationship with God, but with the Church as well. He knew that

---

30 Bishop Fulton Sheen, *Life of Christ*, (New York: Image Books, 1977), 423.
31 Gregory the Great, *Homily on the Gospels* (26, 7-9: PL 76, 1201-1202) in *The Liturgy of the Hours*, Vol. III. (New York: Catholic Book Publishing Company, 1975), 1517.

there is something that occurs when one shares their burden with another; something that lessens that burden. That is why we celebrate in a special way, this: the Second Sunday of Easter. That is what we call Divine Mercy.

THIRD SUNDAY OF EASTER

ACTS 5: 27-32, 40-41; REVELATION 5: 11-14; JOHN 21: 1-19 PSALM 30

"Do you love me more than these?"

The one who first denied "the Name" now is *full of joy that they had been judged worthy of ill-treatment for the sake of the Name. You changed my mourning into dancing; O Lord my God, forever will I give you thanks.* What could have changed Peter's attitude so completely? I believe it to be two major things, among a few others. The first is that this episode in Acts occurred after Pentecost, so they are filled with the Holy Spirit. The other reason is a bit more subtle. But perhaps it would be better first to explain what change Peter experienced.

Follow this dialogue from John and even *we* might be confused (as Peter obviously was) as to why Jesus asks him three times, "Do you love me?" Before we look at the Gospel, however, it is helpful to return to the original Greek in which it was written. In the ancient world, there were four words commonly used in Greek for love. There are two different words used in this dialogue. That can be deceptive because as the dialogue appears, Jesus asks: "Do you love me?" Peter answers, "Lord I love you." The same word in English is used between them. Plain and simple, right?

The first word in Greek is *philios*. *Philios* was used to describe a "friendship" type of love. The second word is *agape*. Agape is an unconditional love. This love, is the love of the Creator. Now, let's look at the dialogue between Peter and Jesus, inserting the proper word in for the English word "love."

Jesus said: Simon, son of John, do you **love** (*agape*) me more than these? *unconditionally*

Peter: Yes, Lord, you know that I **love** (*philios*) you. *As a friend*
Jesus said: Feed my lambs.

Jesus said: Simon, son of John, do you **love** (*agape*) me? *unconditionally*

Peter: Yes, Lord, you know that I **love** (*philios*) you. *As a friend*
Jesus said: Tend my sheep.

Jesus said: Simon, son of John, do you **love** (*__philios__*) me? *As a friend*

Peter: Lord, you know everything. You know well that I **love** (*philios*) you. *As a friend*
Jesus said: Feed my sheep.

There is no misprint in this dialogue. Jesus asks twice for the unconditional *agape* love and Peter just cannot do it. Finally the third time, Jesus decides to meet Peter where he is, to take him by the hand and lead him to where he needs to be. How can we know this? After each statement of "friendship love" Peter offers to Jesus, Jesus will give the prescription to follow in order to grow into *agape* love. This includes feeding my lambs; the ones who are vulnerable and young in the faith. This includes tending my sheep; bringing those who are outside of the fold, into the fold and caring for those who have always remained. Finally, feeding the sheep means giving them the Eucharist, which will nourish them far better than any earthly food. Peter obviously did these things. How do we know?

Because he was our first pope...the first shepherd. And he went from denying Jesus, to being crucified upside down in Jesus' name. Jesus predicts this in his last statement: *I tell you solemnly: as a young man you fastened your belt and went about as you pleased; but when you are older you will stretch out your hands, and another will tie you fast and carry you off against your will.*

We look at Peter, and thank God for him...for he is one like us. He guarded the Sacred Tradition and followed the command of Jesus to *do this in memory of me*, by offering his body and blood wherever he went, until finally he offered his own. Jesus is unwilling to force us to go where we need to be. He will compel us, not with force, but with the love of him which is written on our hearts. We need only answer one question: *Do you love me more than these?*

Fourth Sunday of Easter

Acts 13: 14, 43-52; Revelation 7: 9, 14-17; John 10: 27-30 Psalm 100

He loved us till the end...even when we were unlovable.

Never again shall they know hunger or thirst, nor shall the sun or its heat beat down on them, for the Lamb on the throne will shepherd them. The Lamb will shepherd. Isn't that the most ironic thing you ever heard? It doesn't say a sheep shall shepherd them, but a lamb. The lamb is innocent and unblemished; certainly not old and wise enough to be a shepherd. What kind of sense does it make? He became one of us...he became one of the sheep. He could not save what he did not assume. He was the lamb, not only because of his innocence; not only because we needed one like us, to save us; but because it was a lamb that was sacrificed. It was an unblemished lamb that was necessary for the ransom. We have such a lamb who is both shepherd and sacrifice. We have such a lamb that not only continues to shepherd us, but who gave his life as a ransom for creatures, even though they were undesirable.

There once was a man named George Thomas, a pastor in a small New England town. One Easter Sunday morning he came to the Church carrying a rusty, bent, old bird cage, and set it by the pulpit. Eyebrows were raised and, as if in response, Pastor Thomas began to speak...

> "I was walking through town yesterday when I saw a young boy coming toward me swinging this bird cage. On the bottom of the cage were three little wild birds, shivering with cold and fright.
> I stopped the lad and asked, "What you got there, son?"
> "Just some old birds," came the reply.
> "What are you gonna do with them?" I asked.
> "Take 'em home and have fun with 'em," he answered. "I'm

61

gonna tease 'em and pull out their feathers and make 'em fight. I'm gonna have a real good time."

"But you'll get tired of those birds sooner or later. Then what will you do?"

"Oh, I got some cats," said the little boy. "They like birds. I'll take 'em to them."

The pastor was silent for a moment.

"How much do you want for those birds, son?"

"Huh?? !!! Why, you don't want them birds, mister. They're just plain old field birds. They don't sing. They ain't even pretty!"

"How much?" the pastor asked again.

The boy sized up the pastor as if he were crazy and said, "Ten bucks?" The pastor reached in his pocket and took out a ten dollar bill. He placed it in the boy's hand. In a flash, the boy was gone.

The pastor picked up the cage and gently carried it to the end of the alley where there was a tree and a grassy spot. Setting the cage down, he opened the door, and by softly tapping the bars persuaded the birds out, setting them free.

Well, that explained the empty bird cage on the pulpit, and then the pastor began to tell this story: One day Satan and Jesus were having a conversation. Satan had just come from the Garden of Eden, and he was gloating and boasting. "Yes, sir, I just caught the world full of people down there. Set me a trap, used bait I knew they couldn't resist. Got 'em all!"

"What are you going to do with them?" Jesus asked.

Satan replied, "Oh, I'm gonna have fun! I'm gonna teach them how to marry and divorce each other, how to hate and abuse each other, how to drink and smoke and curse. I'm gonna teach them how to invent guns and bombs and kill each other. I'm really gonna have fun!"

"And what will you do when you get done with them?" Jesus asked.

"Oh, I'll kill 'em," Satan glared proudly.

"How much do you want for them?" Jesus asked.

"Oh, you don't want those people. They ain't no good. Why, you'll take them and they'll just hate you. They'll spit on you, curse you and kill you. You don't want those people!!"

"How much? He asked again.

Satan looked at Jesus and sneered, "All your blood, sweat and tears… your very life!"

Jesus said, "DONE!" Then He paid the price.

The pastor picked up the cage, he opened the door, and he walked from the pulpit.[32]

---

32 Internet Forward.

FIFTH SUNDAY OF EASTER

ACTS 14: 21-27; REVELATION 21: 1-5; JOHN 13: 31-33, 34-35 PSALM 145

Sometimes it is only through suffering that we are finally able to fly.

We must undergo many trials if we are to enter into the reign of God. Theodicy, or the study of why we suffer, is one of the most profound and difficult areas of study. Certainly, no one wants to suffer, and yet it is a part of all life, not just human existence. Why suffering? Paul and Barnabas give one good reason to the people: *to enter the reign of God.* It makes sense. They recognize that people will suffer, but we can accept such suffering or run from it. If we accept the suffering, we can do so with wailing and grinding of teeth, or graciously. I know, you say "graciously!"

The Lord is gracious and merciful, slow to anger and of great kindness. The Lord is good to all and compassionate toward all his works. The psalmist is clearly convinced of God's *Hesed* (in Hebrew) or His abiding love and mercy. How could such a God that makes that promise allow his loved ones to suffer? Because, if we never were permitted to suffer, we might never have the opportunity for an encounter with Him. Easter is a celebration of the victory that suffering brings. A victory that would only be possible through suffering, and the resurrection that follows. That through suffering, to be with our Creator forever was made possible. And that reason alone…is enough.

There was a zoology teacher who took his class into the wild. The twelve of them were looking at the various flora and fauna while listening to the instructor's explanations. One student saw movement out of the corner of his eye and paused a moment to investigate. The rest of the class continued on, as he watched what appeared to be a cocoon. The butterfly inside had made a small hole in the end and was beginning to force its body through the opening.

The student was elated, thinking that he would never see this again. He watched as the butterfly struggled and wriggled in seeming agony and began to force its body through this small opening. After a moment of struggle, it would remain motionless as if it were exhausted. The struggle would then begin again as it squirmed and forced its body through the small opening, appearing to suffer a great deal. Finally two legs emerged on either side, but again the butterfly stopped, and was motionless, perhaps regaining its strength. Finally, with renewed vigor and tenacity it began the struggle again. Well this was about all this student could take. He took out his knife and opened up the scissors. Using the scissors, he then made a small cut into the hole, opening the hole wider, so that the butterfly, no longer constricted, easily emerged from the cocoon.

The student noticed, as the butterfly emerged, that its wings were still crinkled up like aluminum foil, and that its abdomen was enlarged. The butterfly dragged its large abdomen behind it, and batted its wrinkled wings as if trying to take to flight, but they remained useless. The butterfly continued to bat its wings as if trying to extend the useless foils, and dragged its large body around, but it would not fly. It could not fly. It would never fly.

Upon returning with the class, the teacher saw the young man and commented on the genius of God. He said: "It's interesting about these butterflies. They cut a small hole in the cocoon, so that their body barely fits through. They struggle for hours; wriggling and pushing, forcing their body through that small opening. But this is all part of the natural course. You see, eventually the wrinkled up wings emerge, and as the butterfly pain-stakingly forces its large abdomen through the small hole, the fluid from the abdomen is forced through the veins of the wings. This happens so that when after a struggle and some suffering, the butterfly emerges, and with wings outstretched, can take to flight. The transfiguration from caterpillar to butterfly is only the beginning. The real suffering and struggle in the end is what gives the butterfly the ability to fly. Without that; there would be no flight.[33]

It is the struggle that makes flight possible...it is the struggle that makes flight worthwhile. *He shall wipe every tear from their eyes, and there shall be no more death or mourning, crying out or pain, for the former world has passed away.* And like that butterfly ...*See, I make all things new.*

---

33 Internet Forward.

SIXTH SUNDAY OF EASTER

ACTS 15: 1-2, 22-29; REVELATION 21: 10-14, 22-23; JOHN 14: 23-29 PSALM 67

The Glory of the Lord gave it light...

I saw no temple in the city. The Lord, God the Almighty, is its temple... he and the Lamb. The city had no need of sun or moon, for the glory of God gave it light, and its lamp was the Lamb. By nature, most creatures are *phototropic*. This is the term that scientists give for those critters that are drawn to the light. It literally means "light eating". We really are phototropic, in a spiritual sense as well as a physical sense. If you have any doubts about this, look outside on a beautiful day and see how many of us are there. Talk to psychologists about Seasonal Affective Disorder. I would propose that our attraction to light is no accident. Because the "Light" is from whence we came.

The infinite goodness and love of God is like a flame. If we light a church full of candles from the one flame of another, as we do at the Easter Vigil, the original flame is never diminished, but continues to burn brightly. It remains the perfect symbol for the infinity of God. So if we have this natural attraction for the light, why does it seem that so often we veer away from it? The Israelites had the pillar of cloud by day and a pillar of fire by night. Those who got too far away from either, did so at their peril. The same is true today, as we go on pilgrimage.

I know it's difficult to stay on track...trust me; my straight path looks like an electro cardiogram printout. I think we have a tough time staying on track, however, because we become numb to the effects of our waywardness. Let's face it; if we saw the devastating effects of our sin on God and others, it would elicit in us a visceral response.

Take a moment and think about someone you love, who has fallen away from you. Maybe they have an addiction and have tried numerous times, only to fail. Maybe they are bipolar or have some other issues that make them difficult, if not impossible to be around, and so they have distanced themselves from everyone. How about the one who went through a messy divorce and was ostracized from the family? Or perhaps, the one who got into trouble with the law; maybe the one who has had numerous relationships to different people and is a constant worry to those around them.

These are the souls that seem to suck the energy and life right out of us. These are the ones who are needy or don't appreciate the opportunities they've been given; these are the ones who can never get it right, because they are so self absorbed, and think of no one but themselves. These ones…ugh…don't you just hate people like that?

These ones, who never seem to get it right; these people….are US! *Anyone who loves me will be true to my word, and my Father will love him and we will come to him and make our dwelling place with him; He who does not love me does not keep my words…I do not give peace as the world gives peace. Do not be distressed or fearful.* The world gives peace, with a condition. We have expectations of all of these individuals, and yet God never removes his peace or protection from us. He never kicks us out, despite the time and time again we withdraw from him. And he will never leave us orphans. *The Holy Spirit, the Paraclete will instruct you in everything, and remind you of all that I told you.*

We are created in a way that we do seek the light; we are drawn to it; we are phototropic. Luke does not use the name Theophilos (Theo philos) or "God-lover" at the beginning of his Gospel by accident. We are created with a void which can only be filled with the indwelling of the Divine. *We will come and make our dwelling place with him.* We are all the children that never seem to get it right; we are all addicted; we are all recovering; we are all wayward, and that's why the only proper disposition is absolute gratitude for the Father who never gives up on us; and understanding for those who have fallen away from us.

We get so frustrated when those we love never get it right. Imagine the frustration of our Creator, when time and time again we do not learn. We are filled with joy, mixed with a bit of trepidation, when they finally do make a great change in their life. We can have hope and yet grow weary of forgiving; of second chances; of disappointment. We have hope, but cannot experience joy. And yet we can learn a lesson from our father, the God of second chance. Because when He observes a real transformation in us, He is filled with pure joy!

Ascension of Our Lord
(See Appendix V)

Seventh Sunday of Easter

Acts 7: 55-60; Revelation 22: 12-14, 16-17, 20; John 17: 20-26 Psalm 97

Take care of your gift.

Listen to these beautiful words of Christ to the Father: *I do not pray for my disciples alone. I pray also for those who will believe in me through their word, that all may be one, as you, Father, are in me, and I in you; I pray that they may be one in us, that the world may believe that you sent me.* The words are beautiful, and profound. They speak about the vocation of the priesthood, and the vocation of the Catholic who is a member of the Body of Christ. The two of them working together… as one…to bring glory to God.

Not all were "one" from the beginning. We witness the martyrdom of Stephen in the first reading today, and yet at the end, it tells us that they *piled their cloaks at the feet of a young man named Saul.* Yep… that's the same Saul who will become Paul, but not for a little while. And yet, I imagine that the image of Stephen burned itself into Saul's memory for some time. But as much as these readings remind us of our vocation to be the priests and the people of God, it also brings to light that we are not in control of anything that is really important in this world of ours. That it is the Lord who has control over all. If we discover nothing else by reading the book of Revelation, we discover that God reigns over all; from the beginning, to the end.

So what does this mean for us? It means that we have a calling from God, specific to us. But it also means that we are not left alone to fulfill this task. That our Lord has provided us with everything we need in order to fulfill His purpose. We are called to use our gifts entrusted to us and continue to enhance our spiritual life and that of the Church, but not to depend on ourselves so much; not to worry about the things beyond our control so much that living becomes a struggle, or our relationship with God is impaired.

I remember my ordination weekend very vividly. An ordination is much like a wedding, in that there is much planning and preparation that goes into such an event. I didn't want to burden a lot of people with preparations, so I did a lot of the preparations myself. Everything was in place. I did it all myself to make sure that everything would run smoothly. I printed out invitations and mailed them; I lined up the readers and lectors for my first Mass. I made sure I had overnight accommodations near Harrisburg so that nothing would hinder my journey to the Cathedral on the day of my ordination.

The ordination day turned out to be a rainy day. Actually, "rainy" may not quite describe the weather, because for whatever reason, most ordination days in Harrisburg have been rainy. This particular day was not "rainy" it was "monsoon," and I mean torrential downpours. The reception that would follow the ordination was set to be a pig-roast outside under tents that had been erected. It was at the Knights of Columbus lodge, so they could accommodate two-hundred people inside if necessary.

The night before the ordination I was playing with my nephews outside and twisted my ankle. I applied ice, but there was still pain when I walked on it. The cantor called me and said that it "was not working out" with the organist, and wanted me to get another. As if I didn't have enough to worry about, I didn't have time to deal with this. I had the worst night's sleep of my life. I was hot, then cold; I felt nauseous most of the night, and when I finally got up at four that morning all I could stomach was a cup of coffee and a small donut, just so I wouldn't get sick.

I arrived at the Cathedral plenty early, to get things arranged. We met with Bishop Winter from the Diocese of Pittsburgh who would ordain us, and the time was fast approaching for us to line up for the entrance hymn. I looked around several times and didn't see Fr. Geiger. He was the priest of my childhood that I had asked to vest me for the ceremony. During the ceremony, there is a point where the new priests put on priest vestments. They are usually assisted by another priest who holds a special place in their life. The priest I had asked to vest me, didn't show up. This was the first in a long string of events that would shape this day. He ended up telling me later, that he didn't remember me asking. So, on the way out to the procession for the beginning of my ordination, I asked my spiritual director, Msgr. Richardson to vest me, and he agreed immediately.

The ordination was beautiful and everything went according to plan. After the ordination, we offered our first blessing to the Bishop, and following pictures, departed for our individual receptions. I drove down to Lancaster, thinking that I would be greeted by a cast of hundreds…I was the first one there. I had to think for a minute: "Am I in the right place? Where are the cars?" I stood there in my suit, covered by a broken umbrella and waiting for Noah and an ark to pass by. If it did, I might hitch a ride. Soon the cars began to pull in. The banquet hall was open, and the tent and pavilion would provide cover for at least two hundred people, after they walked down the slick stone stairs.

I greeted people as they arrived, and honestly didn't need to fake a smile...I was still in the clouds. As I watched, the people walked down those treacherous stairs and under the tent! What was wrong with these people? Didn't they see the hall was open? They continued down to the tents. In fact, one old lady actually stumbled, did a half somersault and landed on her feet at the bottom of the stairs, only to continue on her merry way (This is not an exaggeration). The cars continued to arrive and the people were everywhere. Did I invite all of these people?! Where were they coming from? They all descended into the swamp which was my reception.

The food was excellent, but the caterer's truck got stuck in the mud. My brother brought his truck down into the "valley of slop" and helped to drag them out. Evening came and morning followed...the first day.

It was Sunday, and my first Mass of Thanksgiving was going to occur at 3pm. It was standard for the newly ordained priest to offer a first Mass the day after ordination. The Mass usually occurred at their home parish, and the pastor would preach. I didn't know Fr. McGarrity, the pastor at the time, very well at all, but since it was tradition, who was I to break it? When I arrived late morning to arrange things, I found out that the air-conditioning was broken. Are you kidding me!? Not only that, but the caterers told me they were two workers short, and they didn't know how they would be able to prepare all the food and serve it.

Most priests have a Master of Ceremonies for their first Mass, but as I said before, I wanted to make sure everything ran smoothly. I wrote out the instructions for the priests, and had trained the servers myself. I had borrowed matching vestments from Good Shepherd church, not knowing at the time that it would be my first assignment as a priest. Several priests who were going to concelebrate offered to be the master of ceremonies, but I told them it was unnecessary. The videographer called and was stuck in traffic, so he wouldn't be able to make the Mass. My brother took the video camera up to the choir loft and began taping.

The Mass went well...in fact it went very well. The cantor and organist sounded great! I didn't understand what the girl was talking about earlier that weekend when she said it was going to be bad. Fr. McGarrity's homily was unbelievable. I still quote it even today. The premise: "You are never not a priest." Wonderful! Then the reception.

I went to the cafeteria, not knowing what to expect and then I saw it. Parishioners, these were people I grew up with, working together with the caterers to get the job done. I know Lee and Dick were back there orchestrating the symphony which was composed of fried chicken, collard greens, sweet potatoes, and cornbread. The food was excellent! I was exhausted...had blessed hundreds of people...an emotional high, and now I was diving, fast. I could barely keep my eyes open to drive home. When I did get home I fell fast asleep. It was only later that I reflected on these days and found the finger of God in every moment!

Of all the ways I could have spent the day before ordination, I spent it playing with my nephews. The spiritual director who vested me said it was one of the high points of his life. My brother was having difficulty figuring out how he could assist. He not only videotaped the first Mass, but helped the caterer the day before to escape the mud bog. I found out that the organist and cantor had skipped my reception after the ordination so that they could practice all afternoon for the first Mass. Out of three-hundred guests, only two people went into the banquet hall at the Knights of Columbus lodge. The parishioners at my parish were trying to find ways to be a part of the event, and the fact that they were needed for the reception after the first Mass was what many of them called "a gift." The Lord calls, and the Lord provides for the one called...sometimes we just get in the way.

I believe Saint Jean Vianney said it best:

Oh what beautiful thing it is to do all things in union with the good God! Courage, my soul, if you work with God; you shall, indeed, do the work, but he will bless it; you shall walk and he will bless your steps. Everything shall be taken count of, the foregoing of a look, of some gratification – all shall be recorded... Oh! What a beautiful thing it is to offer oneself, each morning, as a victim to God![34]

34 St. Jean-Marie Vianney, in *The Cure D'Ars: St. Jean-Marie-Baptiste Vianney*, by Abbe Francis Trochu, (Rockford Ill: Tan Books and Publishers, Inc., 1977), 29.

PENTECOST SUNDAY

ACTS 2:1-11; 1 CORINTHIANS 12:3-7, 12-13; JOHN 20: 19-23 PSALM 104

"And they were all filled with the Holy Spirit."

A few weeks ago I was at Yankee Stadium in New York, with Pope Benedict XVI.[35] Don't get me wrong, I wasn't side by side with him, and I didn't join him for coffee. But I was among countless others who were celebrating with him. The weekend was a glorious weekend, that started out terribly wrong.

I had arrived at the diocese to pick up my ticket, and the person in charge had actually only assigned me a general admission ticket, whereas I was supposed to be a concelebrant. But they said I was on "a list" somewhere, so things should work out. I was told that morning, that I had rehearsal that evening as well. My friend Melanie met me at the train and got me to where I needed to be, as she lived in New York and was street smart to say the least. I got the train on time, and found the apartment of my friend with whom I was staying, and all seemed right in the world. I went to the rehearsal without any trouble, and we all sat down...me, and about two hundred other priests who were to assist at the celebration.

They began to call the names...Arnold, Blaskovich, Booker, I waited patiently...Monroe, O'Donnell, O'Malley; I waited some more. Finally they got to the "R's". Raburn, Robinson, Ross... Sanders... wait...my name was not mentioned. "Perhaps they misspelled it," I thought, so I waited again. They asked whose name was not called, and I did the "walk of shame" along with several others. The only

---

35 This homily was written in 2008, when Pope Benedict XVI came to New York.

difference was, when the others went down, they found their names…I did not.

I waited with one other priest for four hours until the Master of Ceremonies finally told us to write down our information and he would try to get us a place. What?! Try to get me a place? He said if there was trouble he would call me. Saturday passed and there was no call, but I was told that I had to be at the Seminary in the morning by 8am. I didn't know where the seminary was, or how to get there. I knew the general area, so I figured I would take the train as far as I could, and then catch a taxi. What a mess that would've been.

That morning, I got on the *express train*, which wouldn't stop at every stop…however, for whatever reason, this morning it was stopping at every stop. I waited patiently (okay, at this point I waited impatiently) praying that I would have what I needed to get there. At the third unplanned stop, a priest got on the train. He saw me, I saw him, we had something in common, this *koinonia* drew him to sit next to me, and we immediately began chatting. I found out, through this conversation, that years before he had lived in New York and went to this seminary. He knew the bus we could get on, upon leaving the train to get to the seminary; and then how to walk from there the five blocks to the front gate. Amazing…I was saved.

It turned out that I would never have made it, because of the distance and bus route. We would have to pay for the bus, so I reached in my pocket and then remembered I was wearing a cassock. I had left my jacket back at the room…with my cash. All I had was my subway pass. As it turned out (which I didn't know at the time) the subway pass also works for the busses. We got to the seminary and waited. We sat around for another two hours and they went through the names again… this time I heard mine…butchered, and only a semblance of my real name, but mine nonetheless, and I was to be down on the field. I was to be one of the priests who would approach the altar during the consecration.

I took the bus ride to the stadium and passed through security, virtually unscathed. I sat in my seat awaiting the arrival of the pope, and already emotionally exhausted from all I had gone through to get here. I was thinking about the *mess up* back home; the purgatorial waiting room at the practice on Friday evening. I thought about the roll call; how many times did I have to raise my hand to say they didn't call my name. I was the only priest here from the Diocese, save for the Bishop. I just didn't want to move, when all of a sudden...

Some music began. And with it, this beautiful young girl in white with some wings on her back (that were the size of cafeteria trays) with satin draped over them. The wind was blowing so fiercely that the satin was wafting up behind her like giant fiery wings...this could not have been planned! Then came the doves...six foot kite doves that dancers were bouncing up and down on the air...and then more doves, on long flexible poles that were darting through the breeze; then twenty more, then fifty more, then hundreds of these doves. And as the music reached the crescendo, about two hundred real doves were released...they circled the stadium twice and then ascended into the sky. Everyone was breathless...which was the perfect condition for a Spirit to enter in.

This was Pentecost. It required an emptiness. "The fruitful kind of emptiness is that of a nest, which the dove of the Holy Spirit can fill, or the emptiness of a flute, through which the breath of the Holy Spirit can pipe the joyful tunes of being one with Christ."[36] This experience was also an exercise in trust, which required not only faith on my part, but work. It required that I do all in my power to fulfill the will of God and to trust that He will only do the very best for me. Paul says: *To each individual the manifestation of the Spirit is given for some benefit.* And yet, He allows us to benefit from such a gift as well.

The experience of the Doves, that preceded the manifestation of the Holy Spirit through the Consecration by our Holy Father... was a moment that affected everyone there, just as in the Acts of the Apostles...regardless of language, race, origin or history...everyone was affected. The only moment that surpassed even that was the reception of the Eucharist. Our Lord Jesus made his dwelling within us through his Eucharistic body and blood. Amazing, that we

---

36 Bishop Fulton Sheen, *The Priest Is Not His Own*, (San Francisco: Ignatius Press, 2005), 101.

experienced the Holy Spirit, just as he did; and then received his body and blood.

That day, for a moment we all call the Mass, time stopped and we were all united...*many gifts but the same Spirit*; a foretaste of the things to come. Is it any wonder that the fruit of the Holy Spirit is Joy? And just think...we have that, not just today, but every time we celebrate together. What a gift. Take care of your gift.

Seventh Sunday in
Tempus Per Annum

1 Samuel 26: 2, 7-9, 12-13, 22-23; 1 Cor 15: 45-49; Luke 6: 27-38 Psalm 103

Turn a cheek, transform a heart.

The bar is raised pretty high today. Here is David in Saul's camp. Now keep in mind, Saul had been pursuing David to kill him on several occasions. Now, David has Saul within his grasp. He doesn't even have to do the killing; and yet, he spares Saul's life. Just think how easy it would have been. No more paranoia; always looking over his shoulder. I mean, we talk about having enemies…but Saul…now there was an enemy; and yet because David spared his life, Saul never pursued him again.

As if that's not enough, Jesus raises his own bar pretty high today. Offer your cloak, turn the other cheek, if they take one thing give them another. Begins to make us think it is too much to take. Make no mistake though, Jesus was neither naïve, nor a "head-in-the-clouds idealist. To make this point, he includes within his talk one phrase. This phrase would have been recognized by the first century Palestinians, who would have thought for a minute and then said, "ahh." To turn the other cheek.

We interpret this statement by our own standards, and yet, it meant something else in an *honor- shame* society. You see, in the first century, Palestine was occupied by the Romans. The Jews, then were the slaves, while the Romans were the superiors. Now in the ancient world, everything was done with the right hand. The left hand was *sinister*. So Jesus is saying to these Jews…these slaves "turn the other cheek if *they* strike you." When a superior struck an "inferior" or "slave" they would back-hand them. To turn the other cheek means to offer your left to them as well. At this point the striker has a choice: they can either walk away....or...they will strike with the Palm of the hand. To strike with the *palm* of the hand is how one would strike an "equal." If the striker were to walk away from the challenge, they would lose honor; if they strike with the palm, it might hurt the victim, but they will have been acknowledged as an equal. Jesus is not saying that we must allow ourselves to be walked on; but that we have a certain dignity that can not be taken away.

So what does Jesus mean then? He means that to forgive our enemy isn't implying that we must simply embrace them; or give them all we have. He doesn't mean that we cannot defend ourselves or shouldn't prosecute those who wrong us. What he means is that we need to learn how to "let it go." That sometimes we hold onto these grudges and turn our minds to vengeance in such a way that they become putrid and rotting within us. This condition creates a heart that cannot possibly love. It's like the old adage, "I drink the poison, so you die." It doesn't make sense.

I am the chaplain at Lebanon Catholic School, in Lebanon PA. I regret I cannot make many of the sports events there because of my hectic schedule; however, I did get to see a few basketball games last year. At one particular girls basketball game, a young girl, Jessica, was fouled. This was a nasty foul. The other team was losing significantly and it was nearing the end of the game, so they started playing rough. As our girl hit the floor from this rough foul, I waited to see what she would do. This was the perfect opportunity for a fight, I mean, it was a rough hit. Jessica got up and walked to the line, not looking at the girl who knocked her to the ground. The other team was shouting and jeering at her as she eyed up the rim for a foul shot. The ball left her fingers and sailed through the hoop. Again, she dribbled the ball as she readied herself for the second shot. And again, the opposing team and their fans were shouting and jeering at her. The ball left her hands and she made a second shot. The crowd cheered as the stands for the opposing team grew quiet. She turned away from the girl who hit her and ran to the other end of the court to assume defensive positions… smiling all the way.

The one who hit her dropped her head, embarrassed to be there. She had dishonored herself, and her team. If Jessica had retaliated, this girl could have saved her honor, but because she did not; because she played by the rules and made her shots; because in that moment *humility* dictated her actions, she was exalted that day. *To be able to let it go.* It seems nearly impossible. We think, "If I let go…if I forgive them, then they've won." The fact is…if we do not forgive them…. if we allow this hatred to grow as a cancer within us; then, they *have* won indeed.

EIGHTH SUNDAY IN
TEMPUS PER ANNUM

SIRACH 27: 4-7; 1 CORINTHIANS 15: 54-58; LUKE 6: 39-45 PSALM 92

What do YOU hold?

Jesus speaks of a blind man leading the blind. There is a story of a blind man, I heard years ago, which is different from any other.

There was a king traveling with thousands of soldiers, who was enroute to conquer another country. He had conquered dozens already, so this was just another effort to pillage and take over. As he was traveling at the head of the brigade, he spied a small hut up ahead on the beach. Typically, he would simply roll right over whatever was in the path, but he saw something very peculiar hanging from the roof of the hut. As he got closer, he was captivated by this object. It drew his gaze, so much that he forgot where he was going, and to what end were his travels. As he drew closer to the hut, he began to see very clearly the exquisite beauty of the piece of pottery hanging from the roof, and in an instant, he held up his fist, and the many legions of soldiers stopped in their tracks. He dismounted and removed his helmet. His head was cocked to one side, like the old RCA dog, as if he were trying to adjust his sight, so beautiful was this treasure.

He approached the shack, still hypnotized by the treasure and walked through the door, which was ajar. There he saw an old man hunched over a potter's wheel, making more vessels like the one he was so captivated by. The old man knew he was here, and before he was able to greet him, the king spoke: "How is it, that an old man who cannot even sit up straight can create such treasures? I have conquered many nations and have possessed countless treasures, but these vessels have a beauty, the likes of which I have never seen." The man now faced the king...he was blind. The king fell to his knees now and spoke once again. How is it possible...how can it be that an old man...an old blind man can create such treasures?" The man smiled and replied: I imagine what the vessel will hold...and then the clay shapes itself."[37]

A good tree does not produce decayed fruit, any more than a decayed tree produces good fruit. Each tree is known by its yield. A good man produces goodness from the good in his heart. "I imagine what the vessel will hold...and then the clay shapes itself." Sirach says: *The test of what the potter molds is in the furnace.* The question, therefore, is not: "How is it possible that someone could form such beauty?" "I imagine what the vessel *will hold*...and then the clay shapes itself."

At this Liturgy, we receive our Lord in the Eucharist. If we allow that to become a part of us, then it will shape our lives. It will shape what we say and what we do; how we treat those we meet; what enters our mind through the various media we expose ourselves to and what grows in our hearts. But...this vessel can only receive our Lord in the Eucharist if it is not filled with something else. If it is already filled, then that with which it is filled will shape our lives; what we say and do; how we treat those we meet and what is permitted to pollute our minds and hearts. Therefore, it is necessary to answer one question. "I imagine what the vessel *will hold*...and then the clay shapes itself." The question is... "What do *you* hold?"

---

37 Internet Forward.

Trinity Sunday

Proverbs 8: 22-31; Romans 5: 1-5; John 16: 12-15
Psalm 8

Exalted in Majesty, undivided in Splendor

An ordinary simple Christian kneels down to say his prayers. He is trying to get into touch with God. But if he is a Christian he knows that all his real knowledge of God comes through Christ, the Man who was God...that Christ is standing beside him, helping him to pray, praying for him. You see what is happening. God is the thing to which he is praying...the goal he is trying to reach. God is also the thing inside him which is pushing him on...the motive power. God is also the road or bridge along which he is being pushed to that goal. So that the whole three-fold life of the three-personal Being is actually going on in that ordinary little bedroom where an ordinary man is saying his prayers.[38]

Trinity is an adjective. The term is never mentioned in scripture because of that. The noun is God, the particular subjects are Father, Son, Holy Spirit. Trinity is an adjective. An adjective that speaks to relationship. Jesus says that *the Spirit I send will teach you and remind you of all that I said.* If Divine Revelation were instantaneous, then we would not need the Spirit to go any further in teaching. Because we are constantly growing deeper in the faith, not like a circle but a spiral, we come to discover more about the truth of God every day. We can see this journey unfold in the ancient errors, called *heresy*, regarding the Doctrine of the Trinity. And if we look closely at these errors called, *heresy*, we come to discover how easily we can fall into the trap.

---

38 C. S. Lewis, *Mere Christianity*, (San Francisco: Harper, 1972), 163.

These errors usually form because of extremes. St. Augustine said: "Virtue is in the middle." We believe that Jesus is "my brother" or "my friend" but not my Savior. This puts us on equal par with Jesus. We are his "adopted siblings" only in so much as we are children of God. We are his relatives, only in so much as he says that *those who hear the word of God and listen to it… these are my mother and brothers and sisters.* We come to see Jesus as a great teacher and also a "son of God" so to speak, but as being nothing more than we are. This is a *Monarchianistic* point of view, the Jesus was a man gifted with divine powers as opposed to *Docetism*, that professes Jesus only "seemed" human. The humanity and sufferings of Christ were seen as "apparent" rather than real.

Another extreme, and one that came up when the Eastern Church split from the Western Church, is *subordinationism.* This says that the three persons of the Trinity are not equal, especially when referring to the Holy Spirit. That the son is subordinate to the Father, or the Spirit is subordinate to both. The issue was that the Holy Spirit was not stressed nearly enough, as well as the gifts and fruits that we receive from the Holy Spirit. The Father pours forth all He is into the Son who returns everything to the Father, and the love between them is so great, that it is manifested in a Holy Spirit. The Holy Spirit is the spouse of Mary, and the Father of Jesus. *She conceived through the power of the Holy Spirit. And the Spirit like a dove descended on him. And a voice was heard from Heaven: "This is my beloved son, with whom I am well pleased."*

This *subordinationism* also applies to Jesus. We spoke of *Docetism,* or that Jesus "seemed" human, but there was also *Arianism,* which exists even to this present day. Arius believed that Jesus was an exalted creature. He was created by the Father. Jesus was somehow divine, but was not God. This is similar in a sense to Islam, where Mohammed is held as divine. What's interesting is that Mohammed did not take on divine characteristics until two centuries after his death. An Arian point of view would make Jesus unequal to the Father and the Holy Spirit.

I know this is a bit much for a homily, and probably a little deeper than we want to go in this arena, however, I think it's important. Why? Because we are surrounded by many churches (referring to the building or assembly of people, as opposed to "the Church"). Many of these communities are drawing our people away, because they are entertaining or community focused or people focused. The religion they teach, however, is often a *Docetism, Arianism,* or *Subordinationalism* of some type. If you don't know these things, at best you won't be able to combat them when your family or friends get drawn into it; at worst, you might fall into the trap without any means to free yourself.

We profess belief in the Triune God in the creed, every time we celebrate the solemn Mass. We believe in one God, and then profess, Father, Son, and Holy Spirit. Our God is so filled with love that it would be too much for one person, and so there are three. Three persons permeating space and time, spacelessness, and timelessness, in one concerted effort...our salvation. What a wonderful faith we have! Who would not want to be a part of something so great? It is important, however, that we learn as much as we can. And don't worry. Jesus promised to send the Spirit, just for this task. We do what is within our power to learn all we can, *and then the Spirit will give you words and wisdom that no one will be able to refute.* We need only ask.

FEAST OF CORPUS CHRISTI

GENESIS 14: 18-20; 1 CORINTHIANS 11: 23-26; LUKE 9: 11-17 PSALM 110

We celebrate today the feast of Corpus Christi, the body and blood of Christ. Benedict XVI says in *Sacramentum Caritatis*: "All of the sacraments and indeed all the ministries and works of the apostolate are bound up with the Eucharist and are directed toward it."[39] He goes on to say: "The church herself is a sacrament. The Church, in Christ is a sign and instrument of communion with God and of the unity of the entire human race."[40] What we have in the Catholic Church is much more than some gift from God...we have THE GIFT from God.

Everyone is in search of "the real." No one likes imitations. "Is that home-made?" Are you using "real, hard-wood?" "Is that authentic?" "Did you see him live in concert?" Even with our sports, when we find out someone is using drugs to enhance their performance, or find out that a singer is actually lip-syncing to the words, we feel cheated or short changed. No one, if asked whether they wanted imitation or real, would choose the imitation. We desire what is real and true and good, not some cheap imitation; not something fabricated or made to seem real.

In the fifteenth century, our Church went through a disastrous division. An Augustinian priest by the name of Martin Luther, saw that there were abuses in the church. Some of these he mentioned had to do with *indulgences* which were being sold at that time by various priests and bishops. He disagreed with the role of Latin in the Mass and wanted the common language of the people to be used.

---

39 Benedict XVI. *Sacramentum Caritatis*, (Vatican City: Libreria Editrice Vaticana, 2006), #16.
40 Ibid., #16.

He thought that the Eucharist was so important, that we should offer it more frequently and under both species (host and cup). What you might be surprised to discover is that he never wanted to split from the Catholic Church; and that he never wanted a reformation.

Martin Luther was the last monk to leave his monastery, and when he did, he still wore his habit and had the tonsure shaved into his head. He has some of the most beautiful essays on the blessed Mother and the saints, and if you read his writings, there is no doubt that he believed in the Real Presence in the Eucharist. So what happened? Well, Pope Leo wouldn't give him a hearing, but the German princes would. You see, Germans Catholics were leaving their land to the Church when they died, and the Church was becoming a major landowner. This "priest" with his complaints would receive the push he needed from these princes. He nailed his ninety-five complaints to the door at Wittenberg, and then it was pretty much out of his hands. The Lutheran church arose and took over.

Now, with some of the trail blazed leading away from the Church, John Calvin led the Calvinist assembly in Geneva who took made their own modifications of Catholic faith; and from there we now had churches named, not for saints, but for founders or "styles of religion." Since western and northern Europe were splitting off, many others joined in the separation, not in an effort to find truth, but in an effort to *marry more wives.* From that tradition, other assemblies sprang into being. Meanwhile…Martin Luther is spinning in his grave!

Jesus said to them: "You give them something to eat." And taking the five loaves and the two fish he looked up to heaven, and blessed and broke them, and gave them to the disciples to set before the crowd. And all ate and were satisfied. Sounds kind of like Paul's letter to the Corinthians: *He took bread, and when he had given thanks, he broke it, and said, "This is my body which is for you. Do this in remembrance of me."* so how do we know? In Lebanon alone there are hundreds of churches, many on one street. So what do we have that they do not? WE have the Eucharist…the center of our faith.

Some might comment, "I thought the center of our faith was Jesus?" EXACTLY. Only in the Mass does Jesus transform bread and wine into the "Bread of Life and the Cup of Eternal Salvation." The Lutheran community does not have that; the Methodist community does not have that; the Anglican community does not have that; the United Church of Christ, does not have that; the Amish and Mennonites do not have that; the Evangelical churches, do not have that, and the crux is THEY WILL NOT DISAGREE WITH ME!

These other communities have "communion" to which anyone can go, because it is a *representation* of Christ. It is a symbol. Even some of the communities which are closer to us, and say that they have the *presence of Christ* in the "bread" say that Christ is present *along side* of the bread and once the service is over, the bread remains just bread. We do not say Christ exists "with" the bread, we say that the bread is transformed into Christ's body and the wine into his blood.[41]

Our faith is different, because belief in the Eucharist is not "one" aspect of our faith, but THE foundation of it. Belief in the *real presence* of Christ in the Eucharist is the *foundation* of our faith. If he did not give us his body and blood, then what he says in the Gospel today should at best frustrate us and at worse scare us: *I am the living bread that came down from heaven; whoever eats this bread will live forever; and the bread that I will give is my flesh for the life of the world.*

We don't settle for imitations in our life. WE want what is real and authentic and life-changing, not some cheap imitation. There is only one place to get our Lord in the Eucharist. There is only one celebration where we can receive the glorified body of Christ into our own bodies. How do we know? Paul says: *For I received from the Lord what I also delivered to you...*or is St. Paul a liar? We know, because he told us. After he told the first Pope, Peter and the first bishops, the Apostles: *I give you the keys to the kingdom of heaven. What you bind here, is bound; what you loose here is loosed.* And he said: *Do this, in memory of me.*

---

41 This is the difference between the Catholic term *transubstantiation* (bread is transformed into) and the Protestant *consubstantiation* (bread exists alongside of).

Ninth Sunday in
Tempus Per Annum

1 Kings 8: 41-43; Galatians; Luke 7: 1-10
Psalm 117

Sons and Daughters by Adoption

Make no mistake about it, the Jews were the *Am Segulah*, or the *Chosen People* of God. He made many covenants with the people, and they journeyed together through exile and war and peace. Now Jesus comes, and the definition of *Am Segulah* is broadened. He is no longer simply to be the savior for the chosen people, but for the *hoi palloi*, (*the many*) as well. This is good news! It means that there is hope even for those of us who did not have the covenant that Abraham agreed to, or that Moses sealed with God, or that the prophets renewed throughout their tours among the people. This means that Christ has made us all children. This is good news, right? I mean we do want everyone to be saved…don't we?

Solomon prays in the Temple, *to the foreigner, likewise, who is not of your people Israel, but comes from a distant land to honor you, when he comes and prays toward this temple, listen from your heavenly dwelling.* What! This is Old Testament, before Christ, and Solomon is praying that God will hear, even the Gentile. Even the psalmist echoes his sentiments in one of the shortest of the psalms: *Praise the Lord, all you nations; glorify him all you peoples!* The "nations" or ethnoi are the Gentiles. What is he saying? He's saying something that might sound like pre-destination. That we are all predestined to be with God, we need only receive the gift.

I would like to tell you a parable.

There was a family out west who had four children. One was older and the younger three toddlers. As they grew older, the younger ones noticed the older was different. He didn't look like the three or act like them. They began to presume that he was adopted. That was just an observation, but they didn't let it stop there. They began to ridicule him, and alienate him, telling him he was adopted. He remained silent, and withdrew by himself.

Upon reflection, the three also noticed that throughout their childhood it appeared that the father and mother spoiled them, and tried extra hard to please them, and perhaps even loved them more. The three siblings brought it up to the father, and he denied that the boy was adopted. Then they would talk about it around the mother, who also denied that he was adopted. Finally, they took it to such a level that the father could stand it no more. He took all the children aside and had a family meeting. "Your mother and I found out that we would not be able to have any more children. We were devastated by the news and so we decided at one point to adopt. The oldest of the three younger children cried out, "I knew it! All this time you were trying to hide it, but we knew he was adopted. Why didn't you just say it?" The father looked at the floor and replied: "Because I didn't think the three of you would understand. You see, the three of you are adopted. You are brother and sisters, but we adopted you together. And perhaps we were unfair, because we tried to overcompensate, not wanting you to feel different. I guess we failed.[42]

Jesus turned in response to the centurion in amazement. *I tell you, I have never found so much faith among the Israelites.* Isn't it amazing that the ones who appear to be the natural children, are actually the ones who were adopted. Isn't it amazing that the ones who were adopted through the death and resurrection of Christ, seem to forget that fact when faced with those who are not like them; or perhaps those who are coming back into the family.

Jesus is the only natural child of the Father. We are only his brothers and sisters in one way...Divine adoption. As the children

---

42 My Original parable.

created by the Father we rebelled and renounced our inheritance. It was only through an act of Divine adoption that we were reunited with Him. Having been adopted ourselves, could we ever possible look on those who have rebelled and gone away; or those who have only now come to know the Father, as anything less than our very own brothers and sisters? If we can look at them with anything but filial love, then perhaps we haven't really returned at all.

Tenth Sunday in
Tempus Per Annum

1 Kings 17: 17-24; Galatians 1: 11-19;
Luke 7: 11-17 Psalm 30

And he sent them out two by two...

The Lone Ranger and Tonto; Batman and Robin; Thelma and Louise; Inspector Cleuso and Cato;   Starsky and Hutch; Perpetua and Felicity; Paul and Barnabas; Cosmas and Damian...and all the saints. Famous duos throughout history. Jesus was not the first to send them out two by two. He was not the first to realize that we are supposed to journey through this life together.   We were never meant to do it alone. He saw the value in this, having experienced true solitude.

Imagine it...you are the son of God...all wisdom... miracles... a union that no one would ever understand and could never approach. Amidst all of them; surrounded by crowds; and no one in which to confide...no one who would understand. They would try, oh they would try their darnedest, and always they would come up short. Jesus would have to acknowledge the solitude once again. That was a requirement for the son of man...but not for everybody else. No one should have to go it alone.

One of the requirements for any program of recovery is to have a sponsor. This sponsor is the one who journeys with the person through withdrawal and cravings; this is the one they call when the temptation seems overwhelming, and when failure pounces upon the mind and heart of the one who has "fallen off the wagon." Isn't it interesting that even the Church requires sponsors for Confirmation? This is not just some ceremonial nicety but a real, life-long responsibility offered to those who are willing and able to make the journey.

We are all on the road to recovery. Just as an addict is never really "cured" but "in recovery" so too are we. But to take a sponsor necessitates humility on the part of the person in recovery. It is not easy to call someone who is going to *call you to task*...someone with whom you must be transparent... totally honest. But as I said before, no one was meant to take this journey alone.

Jesus sends them out two by two, because that way they would keep each other in check. I often wondered, however, if he counted them off like we did in the old days of "gym class" or if in his great wisdom, he chose the most unlikely couples and placed them together so that they might learn to love each other and work together, knowing that in the days to come they would encounter many more disciples with whom they would have to work. It was not only to keep each other in check, but also to support each other in difficulty. I often wonder when it says *they cast out demons*, if they hadn't spent most of the time casting out each others' demons.

Poor Amos...alone against an empire. The Lord was always with him and yet you can hear the solitude in his voice. How many of us are *Amos* in the world...trying to battle an empire alone, when it was never meant to be like that? Paul refers to the Church as *the body of Christ* for a reason. We are not simply a social club...we are not simply a place together...we are part of something bigger than ourselves...or at least...that was the idea from the beginning. When two work together, it's amazing what can happen. Jesus knew this very well.

Wishing to encourage her young son's progress on the piano, a mother took her boy to a piano concert. After they were seated, the mother spotted an old friend in the audience and walked down the aisle to greet her. Seizing the opportunity to explore the wonders of the concert hall, the little boy rose and eventually explored his way through a door marked "NO ADMITTANCE".

When the house lights dimmed and the concert was about to begin, the mother returned to her seat and discovered that the child was missing. Suddenly, the curtains parted and spotlights focused on the impressive Steinway on stage. In horror, the mother saw her little boy sitting at the keyboard, innocently picking out three notes. Doe ray mi. As the attendant stormed the stage to remove the meddlesome youth, the great piano master made his entrance, quickly moved to the piano, waving off the attendant. He quietly approached the boy and whispered in the boy's ear, "Don't stop playing." Then leaning over, he reached down with his left hand and began to play chords to match the notes the boy was playing. Soon his right arm reached around to the other side of the child, and he added a running melody to the three notes… and a wonderful rhapsody was created. A bunch of notes that seemingly had no relationship at all became a wonderful song in the hearts of those who listened. The audience was so mesmerized that they wouldn't recall what else the great master played that evening.[43]

Because an old master was patient, and the young novice was willing to take a risk, a chaotic assembly of sounds was transformed into a wonderful rhapsody. That night, they heard a composition they had never heard before, and would never hear again.

---

43 Internet Forward

ELEVENTH SUNDAY IN
TEMPUS PER ANNUM

2 SAMUEL 12: 7-10, 13; GALATIANS 2: 16, 19-21; LUKE 7: 36 - 8 :3 PSALM 32

We are teaching our daughters to be like this woman…
We are teaching our sons to be like this man.[44]

Bratz Babyz makes a "Babyz Nite Out" doll garbed in fishnet stockings, a hot-pink micromini, and a black leather belt. To look "funalish" (whatever that means), the baby also sports a tummy-flaunting black tank paired with a hot-pink cap. Dare one ask what is planned for "Babyz Nite Out" and what, exactly, she is carrying in her metal-studded purse?...The dolls are officially for ages "four-plus," but they are very popular among two-and three-year-old girls as well.[45]

As I walked around a crowded city shopping area on a hot day last week, it often felt as though glancing anywhere below head-level in any direction was fraught – yet not doing so could clearly result in a twisted ankle. However, amid the plunging necklines and beltlines, piercings and tattoos, one woman stood out. She was wearing a long white summer dress with a red pattern on it, and she stood out because it made her look …pretty! Remember pretty? Ah, yes – I'd almost forgotten it, lost among all the hot, hip, raunchy grrrl-wear that has become the official uniform *de nos jours.*[46]

---

44 This homily is part of a talk given on Intimacy. The full text can be found in Appendix VI.
45 Wendy Shalit, *Girls Gone Mild*, (New York: Random House, 2007), xv-xvi.
46 Ibid. 138. The translation of the French idiom is "in our time."

We are teaching our daughters to be like this woman. *A woman known in town to be a sinner…stood behind him [Jesus] at his feet, weeping so that her tears fell upon his feet. Then she wiped them with her hair, kissing them and perfuming them with the oil. When the Pharisee, saw this, he said to himself, "If this man were a prophet, he would know who and what sort of woman this is that touches him – that she is a sinner."*

Twice this woman is labeled as a sinner: by the local people and by this Pharisee. No one forced this woman to be there; no one forced her to bring the expensive perfume; no one forced the kisses. She approached the Savior after a lifetime of searching for him. She searched for him in the things of this world, even though she knew it not. She searched for him in the men she encountered, although he would not be found in their hearts. Finally, she searches for him in a place she fears most…a place where her sins are exposed by the one who owns the house. And she kisses the feet of Christ, perhaps the first kiss she's ever offered out of real love for another. *I tell you, that is why her many sins are forgiven – because of her great love. Little is forgiven the one whose love is small.* And this Pharisee, among others, was one of those who made her the person she was. Only Christ could make her the person she became.

How does this happen? We are teaching our sons to be like *this* man…David. Now David is revered among Jews and Christians alike as the great king. He is legendary both for his trials and triumphs. And yet, David in his day, was responsible for cultivating a lifestyle that objectified women. Thus enters Bathsheba. David with his hundreds of wives and concubines (look it up) still lusted! How is this possible? With hundreds (literally) of women to choose from, David still went after the wife of Uriah.

The Lord says: *I anointed you king of Israel. I rescued you from the hand of Saul. I gave your lord's house and your lord's wives for your own. I gave you the house of Israel and of Judah. And if this were not enough, I could count up for you still more. Why have you spurned the Lord and done evil in his sight? You have cut down Uriah the Hittite with the sword; you took his wife as your own, and him you killed with the sword…* What drives a man to do such a thing?

We could blame society, and should blame society, but that does little to change the state of affairs. We need to begin with our own families...we are the head of the household, the *domestic church*, so it must start there. What happens is so often we get lazy, or tired of fighting the world. I can understand that, believe me. But this culture that promotes the objectification of women, and the emasculation of men through sexual dominance, is made up of people who grew tired of fighting.

We must reclaim our innocence. There is an old wives' tale about how to boil a frog. They say that if you're going to boil a frog, don't heat up the water first. If the water's already boiling, as soon as the frog goes in the pot, he'll hop right out again. Put the frog into the cool water and slowly heat it up to boiling. The frog is not sensitive enough to notice the changing temperature, and will remain there, unaware and boil away. How true is that for us!

The temperature is turned up slowly each year. If you doubt this, just consider what's on television these days. Take any of the shows on television right now, and go back thirty years, even twenty years, and try and put it on the television then. Are you kidding me? It wouldn't happen. There would be such an outcry from the public that the show would immediately be removed. There were times in the sixties when the Church spoke out against certain movies, therefore, people didn't go to see them and very quickly they shut down. No doubt, many of us are boiling and we don't even know it.

Now is a good time to make a moral inventory. How are we living our lives? What kind of model are we setting up for our children, who incidentally, look to us in order to learn how to be adults? What are we allowing them to see and hear? And don't fall into the trap of believing it's enough to regulate what *they* do in your house. We can work very hard to ensure that our household is safe and then allow them to spend time within one that is not safe.

We can no longer depend on a society to regulate shows or movies, and you know this if you've gone to a PG-13 movie lately. In the seventies, the rating would have been "R" or even "X" for some of the current films. We have an obligation to form men who love women for their own sake; who wish to grow in love with them, mind and heart so that one day they might be united in the Sacrament and their union would be complete with a physical consummation. We have an obligation to form men who see the beauty in a woman not as something for him to conquer or possess, but as a gift to be cherished and guarded against malice.

We need to form women who are proud of what they can do with their minds and hearts; who are not so consumed with a sexual body that they starve themselves or allow themselves to be used as they search for love. We have an obligation to teach our sons and daughters how to be Ladies and Gentlemen, in a way that empowers them to one day offer themselves to another as an unspoiled gift. We need to show them what true intimacy is about. And we will do this in a most effective way...when we model the behavior; when we live the lifestyle ourselves. When we live in the way we would want our children to live.

TWELFTH SUNDAY IN
TEMPUS PER ANNUM

ZECHARIAH 12: 10-11; GALATIANS 3: 26-29; LUKE 9: 18-24 PSALM 63

Who do they say I am?

Disillusionment can be an awful thing, and yet in the same breath, I need to thank God for the gift. As I was preparing for the Seminary, I had these great visions of grandeur. On one hand, I thought my prayer life would be better than it ever was before; and on the other hand, I thought I would be surrounded by these guys who were so holy and good, without fault or foible. When I arrived I quickly learned that my prayer life was far beyond anything I thought possible, and that of the men I was with here in the seminary, many had "mouths like sailors", and had their own issues and habits that didn't seem like "priest material" at all. I soon came to discover something very real... why would I expect these guys to be so good, when I myself had miles to go toward goodness?

Life is messy! It is not cut and dry; it is not clean and precise and it certainly is not some romantic portrait from a Norman Rockwell painting. If we have any doubts, Jesus paints a stark contrast to the picture that was developing in the mind of his most intimate followers. God's ways are not our ways, and yet through the prophet Zechariah, God promises to give us the gift of sight, if even for a moment. *I will pour out on the house of David a spirit of grace and petition, and they shall look on him whom they have pierced, and they shall mourn for him as one mourns for an only son, and they shall grieve over him as one grieves over a first born.* "They shall grieve as I do." Wow...to experience the sorrow of God...the grief He feels. The purpose of Jesus coming into the world was to reveal the Father to a people who thought they knew Him…to offer himself as a ransom for a people who knew him not.

> There was a blind girl who hated herself because of her blindness. Not only did she hate herself, but she hated everyone else, except her loving boyfriend. He was always there for her. She said that if she could only see the world, she would marry her boyfriend. One day, she was told that someone left their eyes to her. She went through the surgery and miraculously, over time she could see everything, including her boyfriend. Her boyfriend asked her, "Now that you can see the world, will you marry me?" The girl was shocked when she saw that her boyfriend was blind too, and refused to marry him. Her boyfriend walked away in tears, and later wrote a letter to her that simply said. "Please, take care of my eyes."[47]

"The Messiah of God" is what all of them supposed Jesus to be, but their idea was skewed. Their romantic idea of the Messiah was the one created for them in the stories of their elders and the Pharisees of the day. The disciples were not dumb, but disillusioned. And because they entered into this union with Jesus under the auspices of an illusion, they now had to make a fundamental decision…would they continue to remain with "this" Messiah. And this choice would not be an easy one to make. *Can you drink the cup of which I drink?* This decision would affect the rest of their lives.

---

47 Internet Forward.

Thirteenth Sunday in
Tempus Per Annum

1 Kings 19: 16, 19-21; Galatians 5: 1, 13-18; Luke 9: 51-62 Psalm 16

Who are we playing to?

What are we listening to today? A prophet is being called, but has loose ends to tie up. The Psalmist praises all the greatness and love of God in Psalm 16, and yet in the same Psalm, mentions those who worship other gods. Paul exhorts the Galatians to live in the Spirit and in the same breath scolds them for *biting and devouring one another*. Jesus, the Son of God approaches some and they have everything to do, except the only thing that matters. What is going on?

Just as Jesus often used stories to make his point, so I will do.

There is a story of a violinist. A violinist got up before the packed hall in Philadelphia, and began to play. As he did so, the once murmuring concert hall grew silent. And as the first sound cut through the space and the bow cut across the strings, there was no movement; no sound for three hours. The virtuoso played all the ballads they knew, and all the familiar songs, but didn't play from his heart.

At the end, the violinist took a bow and walked off stage. As he did, the crowd erupted in applause, shouting and clapping and roaring for the performer. Off stage, the virtuoso knelt down and began to cry. The stage-hand looking on thought: "He must be so proud." As he listened further, however, he noticed the violinist was actually weeping. The stage-hand said: "What are you crying for? Don't you hear that!? The whole world is on their feet out there. They're clapping for you....that is for you!" The violinist looked up and said: "You're right. It seems as though the whole world is out there... and they're applauding. Everyone is on their feet.....except for one. The woman sitting in the front...she is not standing... she is not clapping... she is my teacher." If the teacher does not applaud, then all is for naught.[48]

It seems we want so badly to listen and we know what is right and good, but we just get off track. Sometimes we allow ourselves to be trapped by our past or regrets; we doubt our abilities or worthiness. At other times, we begin to listen, but then get side-tracked like the Apostles sometimes did. But there is no standing still in the spiritual life. If we are not moving forward, then we're going in reverse. If we become too consumed with our past failings and mistakes, we risk much more.

Foxes have dens and birds have nests...he who puts his hand to the plow and looks back...he who wants to bury his father and mother. Wow...Jesus is speaking of three types of followers. He doesn't want us to enter into anything lightly, but he is not telling us to ignore what we know is written in our hearts as well. Warning, foxes and birds have all kinds of security. They surround themselves with nest and den and family, that is their home base, their anchor in the world. You cannot be anchored in this world.

You cannot be bound by the things of this life. If you are, then one of two things will occur: You will be distracted, or you will never follow in the first place. As the man said: Let me bury my parents, I imagine Jesus let out a sigh and said, "Next please." This guy's parents probably weren't even old yet, but it was a valid excuse. There are plenty of excuses not to follow, and many of them are very good, otherwise we could not choose them; but often they are the easier of the options. The man who puts his hand to the plow has good intentions. But as my Latin teacher used to say, when we "forgot our homework", "Honey, the road to hell is paved with good intentions." Pun intended here! If you're plowing and keep looking back, your lines are gonna be crooked...need I say more.

---

48 Tony Evans. Radio spot

It is much easier to play what the crowd wants to hear, to rest in the security of a den or nest, to excuse ourselves for really good reasons...and yet, in the end, we know that we have not played our heart. In the end, the fruit is tears. Today is a new day. A day to listen and to live what we know to be the truth. The world will applaud at the most abominable things. Anyone can play to the crowd, especially those things they want to hear. But to play what is in our hearts, takes skill; takes patience; takes courage. To play what was written in our hearts from the beginning. So that one day, the master will be the first to stand, and smile, and applaud!

FOURTEENTH SUNDAY IN
TEMPUS PER ANNUM

ISAIAH 66: 10-14; GALATIANS 6: 14-18;
LUKE 10: 1-12, 17-20 PSALM 66

That's why we call him Saint!

May I never boast of anything but the cross of our Lord Jesus Christ!
Through it, the world has been crucified to me and I to the world. May
I never boast. Paul is obviously remembering Saul. One of the most
famed stories in the New Testament is the Conversion of Saint Paul.
This is so true, that we actually have a feast day of his conversion on
January 25th , aside from his other feast. We look on this event as a
turning point, not only in his life, but also in the life and future of the
Church. I would propose, however, that to limit it to a turning point
would not give nearly enough credit to the life of St. Paul, who calls it
a "crucifixion".

Most appropriate, would be to call January 25th, the feast of Paul's
Conversions. Notice the plural ending. Conversion or as the Greeks
called it *metanoia*, means *a turning of the mind.* This is the phrase from
which the secular world gets "changed their mind", but don't expect
them to give the Church credit any time soon. Paul had an experience
of Christ unlike any other ever. And I would venture to say, if anyone
had such an experience, they might not sleep for days, maybe weeks,
and would have such zeal that they would be an unstoppable force in
the world. But Paul was not a god (he was the first to say that) and as
human nature goes, we tend to doubt over time. Paul never speaks of
another encounter with Christ, outside of the Eucharist. And although
he had several inspirations from the Holy Spirit, there is no doubt that
for him, life was a struggle...a struggle to be the Apostle God wanted
him to be.

He goes on to say: *All that matters is that one is created anew.* How does this occur? *Metanoia.* Not a once in a lifetime event, but daily events which require a constant return to our source. Conversion is not for the faint of heart. But before we are apostles and evangelizers, this is a necessary step.

> When Abraham descends from the mountain (Moriah) with his son, both he and Isaac have changed; something has happened on that hilltop…Nothing seems to have changed. But there has been a change. Like a tree which has been turned full circle in the ground, Abraham's roots have been cut loose, and he has returned a new man.[49]

Jesus himself warns us as apostles: *I am sending you out as lambs in the midst of wolves.* If there is no *metanoia* and we are the same people we were before, then we will be fodder for wolves. Isn't it interesting that lambs typically have a fence around them to protect against wolves. Lambs are naturally on the defensive, but that is not what Christ is saying. Christ the "Good Shepherd" is saying, "go get'em." In other words, we are not on the defensive, but the offensive. And all he promises is the possibility that comes with wolves. But Isaiah promises: *The Lord's power shall be known to his servants.* What power is this? The power that comes with conversion of heart. We cannot face God and the evil One at the same time. We will face one and reject the other. *Metanoia* necessitates a movement from the evil One to God. A drastic change in our life. C.S. Lewis puts it another way:

> If I am a field that contains nothing but grass seed, I cannot produce wheat. Cutting the grass may keep it short: but I shall still produce grass and no wheat. If I want to produce wheat, the change must go deeper than the surface. I must be ploughed up and re-sown.[50]

The snakes and scorpions are creatures of the darkness. If we are facing the light, we can see the danger and trample it underfoot. Not because we are stronger, but because we are facing the One who created

---

49 Fr. Peter van Breeman, *Called by Name*, (New Jersey: Dimension Books, 1976), 19.
50 C.S. Lewis, *Mere Christianity*, (San Francisco: Harper, 2001), 199.

the snakes and scorpions. Paul's conversions required a commitment, regardless of the pains and discomforts; regardless of the response of the people. It was why he called it crucifixion; it was how he could say: let no man trouble me, for I bear the brand marks of Jesus on my body. It was why he was the greatest of Apostles…it is why he's called Saint.

FIFTEENTH SUNDAY IN
TEMPUS PER ANNUM

DEUTERONOMY 30:10-14; COL. 1:15-20;
LUKE 10:25-37 PSALM 69

The right question to ask. Who am I a neighbor to?

There are two songs I recall from when I was a child: "Who are the people in your neighborhood" and "Won't you be my neighbor." Two songs trying to answer an interesting question posed by a scholar of the law to Jesus. "And who is my neighbor?" This may seem like an easy question to answer, however, the question is the wrong one to ask.

In the ancient world the neighbor (or *plāsitos* in Greek) was one who was like you. They thought like you; acted like you; voted like you; etc. For a Jew, it would be another Jew; and for a Samaritan, another Samaritan. And so "love your neighbor" is not such a difficult task at all, is it? Which is why Jesus does not answer the question. The question is the wrong question. He does not so much give an answer to the question posed, but instead changes the question.

In the parable of the "Good Samaritan," a Jew and Samaritan meet. These were deadly enemies. In fact, a Jew touching or speaking with a Samaritan would be unclean and be exiled until he went through the cleansing rites. For a Samaritan, it would be similar. This wasn't just a preference or prejudice like the Capulets and Montecues or the Hatfields and McCoys where no one really knew what caused the division in the first place. This division was based on history.

When the Babylonians took the Israelites into exile, they didn't take all of them. Like any good conqueror, they wanted the rich and powerful, the intellectuals, and those who were the ruling powers in Israel. The poor and uneducated they left behind to fend for themselves. During their captivity, there was no temple or Ark of the Covenant, so these "Diaspora" Jews became a people of the Book, or the Law. Meanwhile, back in Israel, the poor and uneducated had no temple cult, because the priests were gone. They had no education, so they could not be a people of the book. So what did they do? Well they moved on with life. They kept their faith the best they could, but mixed with the pagan community. Before too long they were doing business with the pagans and eventually began to worship with them and intermarry.

Well, as all things must come to an end, with Cyrus the Persian the Exiles were allowed to go back to Israel and rebuild. Upon their return, you can imagine their outrage. After their suffering in exile and struggle to keep their faith alive, they return to find their brothers, they had left behind, had "fornicated" or allied themselves with another faith. Needless to say, these "fornicators" were quickly exiled themselves and settled in Samaria. They would forever be known as the Samaritans, and a good Jew could not mouth the word without spitting.

There's the history. I mean this was a real hatred. Recall last Sunday when the Samaritans knew Jesus was heading to Jerusalem, so they would not allow him to pass through. Pretty tough for us to imagine…or is it?

Imagine this. Your eyes meet those of your worst enemy. Think of the one you like least in the world. Maybe the one who rejected you or took advantage of you. Maybe the one who hurt or betrayed you. Your eyes meet theirs just as you are about to undergo a life-saving procedure. They are the Doctor and your life is in their hands. What would you do? How would you view them now? The one you despise. Would you allow them; would you trust them to spare your life?

Imagine your eyes meet those of your worst enemy. You've witnessed a mugging and they are possibly mortally wounded. This is the one who has made your life a living hell. Your eyes meet and you can save them. What do you do? Could you walk away? Would you walk away? I ask these questions because I have first asked them of myself. NO! If we did walk away, we would feel the consequences of that abandonment. Why?

There is something within us that is divine. An indwelling of the Father who wished that none of His children should be lost. As Moses says: *This is not too mysterious and remote for you; it is not up there in the sky, or deep in the sea; it is engraved on our hearts.* But either we can't find it...or have buried it so deep in regret or resentment or fear that we no longer recognize it.

Paul says: *We see in Christ the image of the invisible God.* If we want to know how we're supposed to be, we need only look at Him. Therefore, Jesus will not answer the question "Who is my neighbor?" because it is the wrong question to ask. Who shows concern even for a bitter enemy?

By the man's standards, his neighbors were those like him...the priest...the Levite. But by God's standards, the one who loves; even when it seems impossible, is most like a neighbor. We do not choose our neighbors, but we can choose who we are neighbors to. On this Holy Feast, let us ask ourselves, "Who are we neighbors to?" What parts of my life am I without because I have shut certain ones out who do not think or act or live as I do? *That,* is the right question to ask. And let us ask for God's mercy on *us* and His grace for us that we might, "Go...and do likewise."

SIXTEENTH SUNDAY IN
TEMPUS PER ANNUM

GENESIS 18:1 – 10; COL. 1:24 – 28; LUKE 10: 38-42
PSALM 15

The most important thing…

"I expect to pass through this world but once; therefore any good that I can do or kindness I can show to any creature, let me do it now… for I shall not pass this way again."[51] Is this kindness simply something we can do? Or something we MUST do? In the ancient world of the Near East (and even today there) one of the most important principles was hospitality. So important was it, that if you and your wife had guests, the two of you would surrender your bed and sleep on the floor. So important was it that if there was very little food, you would go without while your guests were nourished. Is this just hospitality? Just optional? NO, this is charity.

Abraham is bending over backwards to accommodate strangers. Why? Because he sees in them the image of God; the presence of God. Paul says: *I fill up in my flesh what is lacking in the affliction of Christ.* Can anything be lacking in the affliction of Christ? NO. Nothing was lacking in Christ's suffering but the lack of afflictions Paul speaks of is in his body. And yet he is striving to fulfill the command given to him by Christ…Charity.

Charity requires that we focus on the *person* and not the *thing*. It requires we take off our blinders and look beyond ourselves to those around us. To stop all the activity and things we're doing and focus on what really matters….people. See, Martha was doing exactly what she was supposed to be doing by Ancient Near East standards. She was

---

51 Stephen Grellet, 1773-1855 (French-born Quaker Minister).

serving, but became so fixated on the details of "doing" that she forgot the one she was doing for.

I was at seminary in Latrobe; about three hours from here. I had an appointment back at the Diocese and was racing after my last class to get there on time. I had made great time on the turnpike, and would even have a bit of time to get something to eat before the meeting. As I was traveling, I saw a car with a flat, off to the side of the road. The woman and her kids were sitting up on the bank of the highway, helpless. I thought, "I don't have time for this today. I have a meeting; people are expecting me. We're planning the Eucharistic congress, etc." As I sped by them, I looked over, and it was almost as though the woman was looking right at ME.

Well, guilt pressed the brake pedal so I pulled over on the shoulder, and carefully backed my way to her car. I raced out of my car and the woman practically hugged me. She began to inform me of what I had already observed, and I began frantically jacking up the car and replacing the tire. She kept talking nervously and obviously could sense my dissatisfaction with this predicament. I was speechless the whole time, just trying to get the thing changed. Finally it was finished. She wanted to pay me but I had no time for this. I said goodbye and raced to my car to get on my way.

As I glanced in the side mirror to pull out, I saw her running up to the side of the car. "Oh great," I thought. She motioned for me to roll the window down and then informed me that on her radio, she had just heard that a milk truck had turned over in one of the tunnels and the turnpike up ahead was closed. She advised me to take the next exit, and told me the "back way" around so I wouldn't get lost. I arrived at the meeting with no time to spare. Like most meetings, it started a little late. I thank God that I wasn't dressed as a priest that day…but the lesson…priceless.

How often do we get so fixated on projects, organizations, fundraisers, or campaigns that we forget what first motivated our zeal; we forget the ones we serve; the ONE we serve. Let us re-evaluate where we are today with our families, friends…the people we touch in our lives and encounter daily. That if we pass this way but once, we might leave charity in our stead.

SEVENTEENTH SUNDAY IN
TEMPUS PER ANNUM

GENESIS 18: 20-32; COLOSSIANS 2: 12-14;
LUKE 11: 1-13 PSALM 138

Teach us to pray

Lord, teach us to pray. This is really the only thing that the apostles specifically asked Jesus to teach them. I imagine, part of the reason was because of their idea of prayer. Perhaps they prayed as I did when I was little.

> I remember I always wanted to fly…well, forget fly, I wanted to be *Superman.* I had made a costume when I was younger (of course I made it) and prayed one night: "Lord, if I sleep all night under this cape, then in the morning please give me the ability to fly." I really, truly believed that would happen, with all my might. I woke up at some point in the middle of the night to go to the bathroom, and there was the cape on the floor. I had not made it through the whole night. I would never fly…unless, there was another way perhaps.[52]

Sometimes, it just seems impossible to pray. We're too tired or too busy, or just don't see the point. We're distracted or restless and just don't find meaning in it. How can that change? What is it that could make prayer productive? Maybe that's the problem. Prayer is not like many of the other things we do or are judged by in this world. Most people see worth, or things worthwhile, in the product that is produced. There is no product in prayer, and so "we must resist the

52 Anthony W. Strubel and Michael W. Rothan, *Home Free* (Indiana: IUniverse Publishers, 2009).

temptation to make prayer productive."[53] Know that if you do pray, it is only because God has invited you and has been waiting desperately for your response.

We are in good company, then, with the Apostles. Imagine seeing the one everyone is saying is the *Son of God*, praying. A father / Son dialogue for hours…on his knees, all night. Think back… "When was the last time I was on my knees, outside of the Mass, praying? When was the last time, outside of Mass, that I prayed?!" If we can answer those questions, then consider this possibility. Parents: What if the life of your child, was dependent on your prayer? Children: What if the life of your parents or family or friends, was dependent on your prayer? Imagine how strong that prayer would be? Imagine the graces you and your loved ones would receive. Even Abraham is praying as if the lives of the people of Sodom and Gomorrah depend on it. And the only people he knew there were Lot and his family. Putting himself out on a limb for a bunch of gravely sinful people, was what Abraham was doing.

We might wonder sometimes if God hears us, and perhaps we wished he couldn't. Because God only helps us to do what is best for us. Remember, he is not the father who would *give his son a scorpion when he asked for an egg; or a snake when he asked for a fish.* C.S. Lewis tells a great story about prayer and why we sometimes do not pray as we should, or don't accept the offering of our Father who knows what is best for us. He writes:

> When I was a child I often had a toothache, and I knew that if I went to my mother she would give me something which would deaden the pain for that night and let me get to sleep. But I did not go to my mother – at least, not till the pain became very bad. And the reason I did not go was this. I did not doubt she would give me the aspirin; but I knew she would also do something else. I knew she would take me to the dentist next morning. I could not get what I wanted out of her without getting something more, which I did not want. I wanted immediate relief from pain: but

---

53 Rev. Peter Van Breeman, *The God Who Won't Let Go*, (Notre Dame, IN: Ave Maria Press, 2001), 12.

I could not get it without having my teeth set permanently right. And I knew those dentists: I knew they started fiddling about with all sorts of other teeth which had not yet begun to ache.[54]

When we call on God for treatment, He will answer, but with a much bigger "YES" than perhaps we wanted. So we try to bargain, not unlike Abraham. But we cannot bargain with a father who wants the best for His children. We cannot ask our Creator to allow us to destroy ourselves, where those teeth are hurting, for fear that we might suffer more in the long run. Paul says: Even when we try to commit spiritual suicide in the flesh, God raises us up again and again and again. *Even when you were dead in sin and your flesh was uncircumcised, God gave you new life in company with Christ.*

God will always grant our prayers spoken in Jesus name which means according to His will. But God waits patiently for us to stop or slow down; to spend some time on our knees in silence and to pray as though our life; as though the life of our family and friends, depends on our prayer…because when you get right down to it…it does.

---

54 C.S. Lewis, *Mere Christianity*, (San Francisco: Harper, 2001), 201.

Eighteenth Sunday in
Tempus Per Annum

Ecclesiastes 1:2, 2:21-23; Col. 3:1-5, 9-11; Luke 12:13-21 Psalm 95

God gives to the needy, not the greedy.

Take care to guard against all greed. For though one be rich, one's life does not consist of possessions. For as Qoheleth says: *What profit comes to a man from all the toil and anxiety of heart which he has labored under the sun, if all his days are occupied with sorrow and grief? When even at night his mind is not at rest. This is Vanity.* But this greed not only manifests itself in possessions, but also a reluctance to share one of the most valuable things we possess; something which, once spent, we can never recapture again....Time.

Paul talks about this as the *greed which is idolatry,* and so we can see it in two ways. I gave up watching television about ten years ago now. Although I rarely had time to watch anyway, there were shows that essentially controlled my life. I would revolve my schedule around certain time frames so I would be able to see the show I wanted. I know none of you ever do that! Seriously... because now you have *TiVo,* or satellite, etc. I did not. But there was an episode in my life (not on the TV) which sealed the deal for me as far as eliminating television from my life.

I had gone to the seminary, and after a few months away, was returning home for the first time. At the seminary I did not have a television, so I had been suffering withdrawal, at least for the first few weeks. And yet there was a peace there. I was returning home to see friends and family for a few days, but when I got home, everyone was at work. I had an hour or two to kill before they arrived, so I flipped on the TV and there I was. I was amazed in retrospect how quickly I was consumed by this box. So much so, that when my family finally came home from work my first thought was: "Oh man. I was watching this and just getting into it and now I'm gonna miss it. Miss IT! Miss what? This box, with no personality, with canned laughter and cheap exploitation of humans was drawing me away from my whole purpose for coming home. Which was taking me away from those I love most in the world. That was when I said "Enough!" ALL THINGS are vanity…Not People.

The first way this greed becomes idolatry, is in our use of time. I experienced this first hand on my visit home. One of the greatest gifts we have…our time, and I was killing it. I was offering one of my finest gifts to a box that could not love or feel or desire life. It resulted in not being rich in what matters to God.

The second way we tend not to think of what is above and not what is on earth is to fill our days with toil and anxiety and things *TO DO*, as opposed to sharing our life with the people we love. We grow up….and one day look around us and ask, "Who *are* these people?"

So we pray: "I thank you Lord for my nice home and many possessions. I thank you that I am successful and well liked; I thank you for my athletic success or the success of my children in athletics and academics." And God responds: "You paid for that house by shortening your life with too many hours or work and alienated your family in the process. You are successful because you have stepped on other people to get where you are and are well-liked because you lie and compromise your values. You are a successful athlete because you practice all the time but at what cost? Where are your friends? When do you pray? When was the last time you ate at home? Your children excel at all they do , but at the cost of fear and punishment or neglect!

"We become like tourists on a bus passing through gorgeously beautiful country; lakes and mountains and green fields and rivers. But the shades on the bus are pulled down. They do not have the slightest idea of what lies beyond the windows of the bus. And all the time of their journey is spent in squabbling over who will have the seat of honor in the bus...until the journey's end. [55]

Isn't this sad...each in a separate seat; each in their own world. Just trying to get where they're going. Where is our focus? Just look at how much time is budgeted within our life, and the true focus will make itself known. So what now? What can we do? C. S. Lewis says: "We never realize how bad we are until we try to be good."[56] True! We never realize how much beer we drink until we give it up; how much we use the internet until the server is down; how much TV we watch until the power is out. But it is possible, and if you doubt it ask yourself this: "Why do we admire the people who can go without these things?" Do we know the people we live with? Do we know our God who gives us our first breath every morning?

What do we choose, because contrary to what the world tells us, we cannot have it all? What do we choose? Do we choose to offer our time to "some-things" which devour without return; or to "some-ones" who can return love for love; time for time; who together with us create a beautiful symphony which is life.

---

55 Fr. Anthony DeMello, *The Way to Love*, (New York: Doubleday, 1992), 3.
56 C. S. Lewis, *Mere Christianity*, (San Francisco: Harper, 2001), 142.

NINETEENTH SUNDAY IN
TEMPUS PER ANNUM

WISDOM 18: 6-9; HEBREWS 11: 1-2, 8-19;
LUKE 12: 32-48 PSALM 33

Fidem scit.[57]

*The confident assurance
(which is etched in our hearts from our very conception).*

*Faith is confident assurance concerning what we hope for, and
conviction about things we do not see.* Wow...that's a packed statement!
It's funny, when we think about it, how much faith we really do have.
I mean let's face it: we let a restaurant make our food and companies
process what we buy; we let doctors open us up and change parts or
modify what's in there; we let teachers train our kids to be adults; and
we let others work on our cars, invest our money, and build our homes,
all with the faith that they will do exactly what they say they will.
Hmmm...but when it comes to God, our faith is wanting.

People can lie, cheat, steal, abuse, use, etc. God does not. God
does not need to lie, because He is the creator of the truth. If He
doesn't like the truth, He can change it. God does not have to cheat,
because He knows all. God does not have to steal, because He can
create all. God does not have to abuse, because He lacks selfishness.
And yet, we choose to place our trust in the ones who are a far cry from
God. Why? Because we are one of them!

Faith is a confident assurance. It is trust. I will often ask little
kids, "Where are your parents in the middle of the night?" "In bed,"
is the normal response. "How do you know that?" I ask. "Because

---

57 *Know the faith* (Latin).

that's where they are!" "But," I answer, "are you there watching them constantly, to make sure they are there?" (I'm waiting for the day when one of them says, "Yeah.") "No, but I know it." "In other words, you *trust* that they are." "Yeah." That is faith!

I imagine, the reason why we lack such faith in such a God, is because if there is such a Person, then we owe a certain amount of Trust and Obedience to Him. This is not something we can get away from …it's how we're created. So often, though, this priority is last on our list of things to do. It is certainly innate within us, and yet sometimes we can deny something for so long, we begin to believe otherwise. How do we know that this desire for something beyond our world is real? How do we know that people do have within them this inner desire that the Psalmist speaks of when he says: *Our soul waits for the Lord, who is our help and our shield?*

Remember "9/11"? How can we forget? I was at the seminary and walked up to the first floor to get some more things out of storage, for we had only returned for the school year weeks before. I looked on the television and saw the jet going through one of the towers and presumed it was a movie they were watching, until I saw the scrolling text at the bottom of the screen, pretty standard for news channels these days. Slowly, I sat down on one of the chairs and watched as well, forgetting where I was, and what I had to do that day. I will remember that day forever, as I am sure many others will as well.

What struck me that day, however, were the effects of such a catastrophe. People have always been very good at coming up with excuses not to go to church. They will get up early to go fishing or hunting; they will pack a stadium after driving six hours for a three hour sporting event or concert, with no complaints; they will shop for hours on end, never tiring regardless of how long they wait in line, or how far they must drive; but they cannot get to Mass on a Sunday morning; they cannot travel to a church less than twenty minutes away, or spend one hour in a service. But…

On September 11, 2001 the churches were packed. It was like it is at Christmas and Easter for those who only come once or twice a year. The people did not flock to the stadiums or the shopping malls;

they did not go to the concerts or movies. It was universal: everyone went to the churches. Whether they were Catholic or not; atheist or humanist; whether they had been away for years or only a few days, they went in droves…they went to see God. Not because they wanted to thank Him, or that they had a spiritual conversion earlier that day. They went because they were scared…and something within them shouted with the Psalmist: *See, the eyes of the Lord are upon those who fear Him, upon those who hope for his kindness, to deliver them from death and preserve them…the Lord who is our help and our shield.*

That day was a wake-up-call for the world. Jesus warns us, despite our faithlessness, *be on guard, therefore. The Son of Man will come when you least expect him.* "The Church is the place of encounter where God meets us and we find God. It is her task to open up a world closing in on itself, to give it the light without which it would be unlivable."[58] There is something within us that desires to trust in more than this world can provide for us. There is something within us which beckons us to approach the Divine. There is something within that leads us to the One who will bring us to fulfillment; the One who can make us feel truly alive; safe within the arms of a Father who is not reluctant to give, and desires only that His creatures trust in Him. But still we fear.

There is something within us that points to the Master. After all, that is how we are made. If you have any doubt, put your faith in what eyes see. Even from a catastrophe came opportunity …and perhaps some of those souls who approached our Lord for the first time almost a decade ago, continue to do so with confident assurance today…perhaps.

---

58 Joseph Cardinal Ratzinger, *Images of Hope: Meditations on the Major Feasts*, Translated: John Rock & Graham Harrison, (San Francisco: Ignatius Press, 2006), 31.

TWENTIETH SUNDAY IN *TEMPUS PER ANNUM*

JEREMIAH 38:4-6, 8-10; HEBREWS 12:1-4; LUKE 12:49-53 PSALM 40

*What **do** you believe?*

We need to be offensive. That's not the best, most politically correct, thing to say mind you…but it's true. We need to be offensive. I recall a date I had at one time with a girl from my town. We went to this restaurant with her friends, so that I could get to know them. We were in mid-meal and one of her friends asked: "What do you do?" I told her I was a teacher. She then asked where I taught. I said St. Leo the Great. She then asked: "Is that a Catholic School?" to which I replied yes. And then she said something which threw me for a loop: "Don't Catholics have all kinds of weird beliefs?"

In Logic, this is what we call "begging the question." It's asked in a way that tells you what the expected answer should be. Now I had a choice here. My first inclination was to kinda' laugh it off, and say, "Yeah, we do have some strange beliefs." But something within me didn't like that. My faith wasn't simply something I did, it was a big part of my life. My parents taught me this faith; priests and sisters spent countless hours passing it on to me, and many people, even in our present century, died for this faith. So I decided (to the chagrin of my date) to be "offensive." "What do you mean by weird?" I asked.

She began with "saint worship" and went on from there. Although our discussion was keeping the rest of the people engaged, she seemed to be going nowhere with it. So I asked her, "What do you believe?" She was silent. All night I had tried to "silence the

123

demon" and all it took was a question (just kidding about the demon thing…no I'm not.). She couldn't tell me. She knew she was "saved," whatever that meant; and she went to church…sometimes. She then returned the question in a way that presumed I would be just as silent as she. And I have to be honest, for a moment, I was caught off guard. The only thing that came to mind was what I recited every Sunday at Mass. "I believe in one God…the Father the Almighty"…. all the way to the end. You could've heard a pin drop. Then one of the other guys spoke up…. "Wow…that's pretty good. So where are we going tonight?"

Needless to say, I'm not dating her anymore… but that's what I mean. We are so worried about offending people; we're so scared of alienating those around us, that we make our religion something we do in private. We make the public Mass, a private devotion. If you doubt this for a second, how do YOU make the sign of the cross when you pray before meals in public?…Unless….you don't pray before meals in public. We are so afraid of offending people, and yet they will make statues of the Virgin Mary out of dung and call it art.[59] A rock singer will descend to a concert in the pose of crucifixion, while Catholics are mocked by newspaper and media for their "primitive beliefs" and "puritanical morals." And we are not offended?

I'll leave you with a story from Fulton Sheen:

A non-Catholic lawyer was asked on his deathbed by his Catholic law partner of twenty years, "Now that you are nearing your end, how about coming into the Church?" The dying man raised his eyebrows. "If your faith meant so little to you during the twenty years you have known me," he replied, "it cannot make that much of a difference to me now."[60]

Jesus says: *I have not come to bring peace! But Division. I have come to set the world upon itself.* Jeremiah was not thrown into prison

---

59 Metropolitan museum of art housed a piece (not of art) "Sensation" in which the Virgin Mary was pictured, covered in elephant dung, as a statement against the Church.
60 Bishop Fulton Sheen, *The Priest Is Not His Own*, (San Francisco: Ignatius Press, 2005), 63.

because he denied his faith, nor because he was not offensive. If we are searching for the true religion, if we want to know if indeed the Catholic Church started by Christ is the true church, simply "look for the religion that is most persecuted by the spirit of the world, and you will find the religion that is divine."[61]

---

61 Bishop Fulton Sheen, *Lift Up Your Hearts*, (New York: McGraw-Hill, 1950),33.

TWENTY-FIRST SUNDAY IN
TEMPUS PER ANNUM

ISAIAH 66:18-21; HEBREWS 12:5-7, 11-13; LUKE 13: 22-30 PSALM 117

We, should be first.

Isaiah says, *I know their works and their thoughts, and I come to gather nations of every language.* Jesus says, we will pound on the door to be let in, and he will ask… *"Who are you?" I do not know you.* Sometimes, with our attitudes, our remarks and witness, we have ensured that some people will never return to the Church. We go to Mass, we have our devotionals, and then we alienate people and judge them; we condemn them for not being as *we are.* And on our final day, the Lord will recall our self-righteousness and say…*I do not know you.*

How then can we get people back? Are we not to guide others to Christ? Do you remember the time that Jesus encountered that woman and said: "You evil sinner. If you continue to act in that way you will never make it into the kingdom." Or when he encountered the man on the way and said: "How dare you approach the altar of God with all you have done in your life?" Do you remember that? No? I don't either, because it never happened. Jesus never condemned anyone in scripture who was seeking forgiveness. The ones he condemned were those who were self-righteous.

He says, *I come to gather nations of every language.* How are we being the witnesses who will do this? How are we to gather these nations…to draw others closer to Christ? By being first. Yep… we have to be first. We must be first:

To forgive
To ask forgiveness
To help
To love.

We are called to be First in all those ways. Then we need not tell the nations; nag them; berate them for their sinfulness, because they will see something that they are lacking, and begin to crave what they have been missing. Remember when Jesus ran into Zacheaus? This guy who stole from everyone? What did he say...*I will stay at your house today*....despite what all others might think. That changed his life forever.

See, we so often set on correcting everyone else...that we forget ourselves. After Sunday Mass one time, a woman approached me and said: "Father, that was a great homily...*those people* really needed to hear that." I had to smile.... "Yeah...*those people* really did!" WE must be first, and then miracles can happen; we are not penalized for being first...on the contrary, we won't even have to knock, and Christ will open the door, welcoming the good and faithful servant.

There is a story told of an Anglican Bishop on his deathbed. He had his family gathered around him; his closest friends and fellow clergy, and took this opportunity to share a very profound statement with them.

As I got out of the seminary, I was ready to change the world...but the world would not change. When the world would not change, I decided to change my country, but amidst all the secularism, my country refused. So I thought I at least have the power to change my state, or at least my village, but they wouldn't hear of it. Finally, I tried to change my family... and even there my efforts met with defeat.

Now as I lay here, I realize the error of my ways. For if I had only changed my SELF, then perhaps my family might have seen my example and followed suit. And if my village or state saw the example and lifestyle my family was leading, who knows, they also might have changed. And if my country saw the example of our small village or state, then they would know change is possible! And if that could happen...who knows...maybe even the world.[62]

Who knows...maybe even the world. *Me first*...and then the world. God Bless You!

---

62 Internet forward.

Twenty-Second Sunday in *Tempus Per Annum*

Sir. 3: 17-18, 20, 28-29; Heb. 12: 18-19, 22-24; Luke 14: 1, 7-14 Psalm 68

The Humble will be exalted...

There are two messages embedded in this parable of Jesus. The first has to do with what it means to be humble; the second describes the identifying characteristics of someone who is. Don't misunderstand, there is a difference between being a humble person and acting humbly. An act can last but a moment, but the humble person endures.

Conduct your affairs with humility, and you will be loved more than a giver of gifts. Humble yourself the more, the greater you are, and you will find favor with God. Act in humility (a moment) and people will love you...be a humble person, and you will be favored by God. But why? Why should I act with humility when others will not? Hmm, that's a valid question.

It seems of all the things that hinder humility in the individual, it is the concern that they have lost, or that they will get the "shorter end of the stick". Hmm...that sounds sort of like pride. The first angel fell to pride and we have followed suit ever since. The psalmist says: *God gives a home to the forsaken, and he leads forth prisoners to prosperity.* In other words, if we humble ourselves, we gain honor. It is not we who will lose, but have gained through our seeming loss.

There is a story that comes to us from the Revolutionary war. There was a Baptist minister by the name of Peter Miller. He had a community of about three hundred families, right here in Pennsylvania. There was a man in his community who harassed him, both inside and outside of Church. The man was a nuisance who often threatened him and tried to embarrass him in front of his congregation. One day, this man was arrested under the charge of high treason and sentenced to hang. Upon finding this out, Peter Miller left his congregation and walked the sixty miles to where the man was to be hanged. He approached General Washington with a plea for the man's life. General Washington replied, "So you walked sixty miles with the presumption that I would pardon your friend." "My friend!" replied Miller. "He's not my friend. He's my bitter enemy." "Well that changes everything," replied Washington. "A pardon is granted."

Miller then walked thirteen more miles to the place of execution. As he approached the gallows, his enemy shouted, "There he is, Peter Miller. Come to see me hanged. Are you happy? This is what you wanted right?" Peter simply walked up to the executioner and handed him the pardon; after which he silently returned to his congregation.[63]

No doubt that we all experience episodes of humility and can see the power of such a way of life. What's rare, however, is to see a humble person, whose episodes of humility are a constant.

There are two people I can never forget. I was at Shippensburg, when I got to know them, and although in the last few years, have been out of touch, their example of humble existence continues to inspire me. While I was at Ship, Grace Boyle was the floor manager for the dining hall. She was never at a loss for words, and always dressed to the nines, even for being in a dining hall. Every time I encountered her, she responded as if she had been waiting years to meet me; and that was every day, sometimes two or three times a day. But that's not all; she did this for every student or adult who entered there to eat. Who was this lady?! How could she be so positive all the time. And then I met her husband John, and came to understand. This couple was so much in love. They were in love with the Lord first, and then everybody else. They are the ones Jesus speaks of in the parable.

---

63 Internet Forward.

The interesting thing about a parable is that the construction is a story that teaches a lesson, but the story could be true. John and Grace are those people who would invite to the feast those who could never pay them back. Grace was forever baking pies, cakes, etc. and taking them to people who could not provide for themselves. First they gave the person communion, and then the conversation and food. At the time Grace was at the Dining hall, she must have been in her sixties. I can't imagine her age now, but the two of them, although aged, are still very involved in their church, and still do all these acts for others. They know the secret to a long and happy life. The secret is in the last words of Christ from the gospel today: *You should be pleased that they cannot repay you, for you will be repaid in the resurrection of the just.*

To humble ourselves; to live humbly; is to live in peace. Not a peace without valleys or shadows, but one that can see the life-giving water in the valley, and the *Son*, who makes the shadows. It is a peace that gives hope.

Twenty-Third Sunday in *Tempus Per Annum*

Wisdom 9:13-18; Philemon, 9-10, 12-17; Luke 14:25-33 Psalm 90

What is it, that so often obscures our vision?

What is the cost of being a Catholic Christian? I went to the seminary in Latrobe, at St. Vincent's. And if you ever get there, the sight to see is the Basilica. The layout is in the shape of a cross, with the altar in the center. Over the altar, suspended by two cables, is the crucifix and beautiful stained glass and marble adorn the building. If you do visit, however, I would recommend staying overnight, just so you can visit the Basilica after the sun has gone down…because it's a totally different experience.

I often made a holy hour there at night, and at night there are two things illumined in the basilica: the cross suspended over the altar; and then way up high in the apse or back dome was the "Lamb" from the Book of Revelation, seated on the throne with the scroll and seven seals. Around the Lamb are the angels and glory of God.

As I gazed on the Lamb and angels and victory and glory I thought, "I want to be there Lord. Where you are praised all day long, by all. No persecution, no pain, just pure joy. I want to be in that place where there is peace." I was totally captivated by the mosaic, wanting to be there. It was filling my whole line of sight, and yet… something was blocking part of the picture, so I shifted to the left.

As I focused on this vision, the words from wisdom in today's reading explains my thoughts. *Who can know God's counsel, or conceive of what the Lord intends, scarce do we guess the things on earth.* I want to be there, and I pray as the psalmist: *prosper the work of my hands.*

Make it so. I know the foretaste in the Eucharist and the feelings of grace that accompany it now, more than ever; and yet at that time I was struggling. When I had shifted to the left, the other part now was being obscured.

And then, the Lord spoke to my heart. In the glory of that Basilica, God looks down on the marble and the flowers, the art and the windows; he looks on the wood and stone and arches, and says: "These, *I* can create! But I cannot create mercy in a heart that is cold; I cannot create obedience in a rebellious heart; I cannot created generosity in a greedy heart, and I cannot create love where it does not exist...I cannot...I will not."

And I began to discover that God will not do everything. That it is up to us. Jesus offers us the cross. But with that cross comes his Body and Blood. We cannot have Body and Blood without the cross. He says, *you will have glory...with persecutions.* We want the heaven, but not the hell we must sometimes pass through to get there. I imagine all the small inconveniences we complain about; the attachments that we cannot relinquish and the *one thing* that we can offer freely to God for all that He has given to us, we withhold. What is that *one thing* for you?

I believe sometimes we get so close to God. We grow so close in our relationship with Him, only to withdraw out of fear that He might take something away.[64] I continued to look with longing on that mosaic in the apse....the lamb, the angels and the glory, and it finally dawned on me what it was that was obscuring my view. The one thing, the shadow which was blocking my dream....that one thing... was the cross.

---

64 Fr. Peter Van breeman, *The God Who Won't Let Go*, (Notre Dame, IN: Ave Maria Press, 2001), 13.

Twenty-Fourth Sunday in
Tempus Per Annum

Exodus 32: 7-11, 13-14; 1 Timothy 1: 12-17;
Luke 15: 1-32 Psalm 51

This brother of yours was dead, and has come back to life...

Listen to Paul's letter to Timothy: *I was once a blasphemer, a persecutor, a man filled with arrogance; but because I did not know what I was doing in my unbelief, I have been treated mercifully, and the grace of our Lord has been granted me in overflowing measure... You can depend on this as worthy of full acceptance: that Christ Jesus came into the world to save sinners. Of these I myself am the worst.*

This story Jesus tells of the sheep is a wonderful illustration. Listen to his question: *Who among you, if he has a hundred sheep and loses one of them, does not leave the ninety-nine in the wasteland and follow the lost one until he finds it?* Now, we've heard this a million times, and we see the shepherd coming back with the sheep on his shoulders, and it makes a great picture or statue. But let me tell you, when Jesus asked that question, the answer from the onlookers would have been a resounding, "NOT ME!" None of them would leave ninety-nine sheep in the wasteland to go after one. For one thing, these are business men, and shepherds of the first century were often compared to thieves and brigands, not only for the way they treated the sheep, but the way they treated their customers as well. Which is why on more than one occasion, Jesus must distinguish himself as the "Good Shepherd."

Jesus wants them to understand the "Father's love" like that of a "Good Shepherd." One who is not interested in business, but has invested Himself in the lives of His sheep. It doesn't mean He is never disappointed, or won't punish or isn't sad or upset when we stray...

or when we betray Him…or when we leave Him. What it means, is that He loves us so much, that despite what we do, His desire never lessens.

Perhaps it might be clearer to take one of the most famous biblical stories and break it down in terms we can understand. This scripture passage has been named "The Prodigal Son" and yet we might call it something else, if we understood the Father. Imagine your child, or if you don't have children, a child you love, or a person you love dearly. This is someone in whom you have invested your life; your resources; your love. Someone you might offer your life for, in exchange for nothing. Think about that person for a moment.

Now…imagine the day your child (that person) ran away. They were tired of the rules, tired of life, they wanted to start over again. So they left; and you had to let them go. What were you going to do, chase after them? Lock them away in the room forever? They were old enough. They knew what it would mean. They packed their bag and left without a word. And you watched…you stood at the front door and watched as they went over the hill, walking on the road to who knows where. You were hurt; you were angry; you felt betrayed, and you didn't remember how many hours passed before you finally shut the door. There was always that slight hesitation. The fear that comes with closing the door on a part of you, and the hope that perhaps, any moment, they'll turn back and realize the error of their ways. But today, there was no return; today no one came back.

Days would pass, maybe even weeks and a ritual would begin. Every morning you would grab your cup of coffee or tea or juice and open the door once again, just looking down the street in the hopes that today might be the day. The anger left weeks ago, even the feelings of betrayal; but the prayers have never stopped. The prayer started out: "Lord, just help them to be happy and successful," but soon changed as well. The prayer became: "Lord make them healthy and well; please protect them and keep them safe." The days were so long without them; and the nights a desert of solitude.

The prayer became one begging for a life. No longer was it a prayer for return, but a cry of "Lord just let them be alive!" And then…

one day, weeks, months, maybe even years after the departure, you stand by the front door, even then, waiting. And suddenly, over the horizon, comes a scrawny creature shuffling up the road. There is no bag with them, and no shoes on their feet, just a shell of their former self, walking…walking towards you. You swallow hard, and no words can escape. It's all you can do not to run right through the screen door. Before the child even looks up in your direction, you are running barefoot yourself, through the icy patches of frost on the grass. You take the child in your arms and carry them into the house, where you wrap them in a blanket and cradle the bones in your arms. The child looks at you, and begins to speak words of apology or love or regret, but you place your finger over their lips, as if to give them assurance that it really doesn't matter why…but that what is most important is that they returned. Your baby was back with you.

Can you relate to this? All of us should be able to relate to it in one way or another. Not because we are all parents, or aunts or uncles; not because we've ever had someone leave us or betray us, or run away. The reason we should all be able to relate to this story, is because we are that child. That child, is me. That child, is you. Time to come home.

Twenty-Fifth Sunday in
Tempus Per Annum

Amos 8: 4-7; 1 Timothy 2: 1-8; Luke 16: 1-13
Psalm 113

Never will I forget a thing they have done!

There was a story I heard the other day, which might provide a nice introduction for the readings this Sunday.

A college drama group presented an Easter play in which one character would stand on a trap door and announce, "I descend into hell!" A stagehand below would then pull a rope, the trapdoor would spring, and the actor would drop from view. The play was well received. When the actor playing the part became ill, however, another actor who was quite overweight, took his place. When the new actor announced, "I descend into hell!" the stagehand pulled the rope, and the actor began his plunge, but became hopelessly stuck. No amount of tugging on the rope could make him descend.

One student in the balcony jumped up and yelled: "Hallelujah! Hell is full!"[65]

Some might wish that.   I doubt, however, it is true. Isn't it interesting, however, how we look to the future all the time. We are constantly putting things off until a later date. We are a generation of procrastinators.

There was a person who once said, "I would be a great procrastinator, but I keep putting it off." The people poor Amos has to deal with, are

---

65 Internet Forward.

all looking toward the future, while they're living life like they have forever to get things right: forever to oppress the poor, to treat people like garbage, to get their lives in order. A prophet of "doom and gloom" is only such to those whose lives will not merit eternal life. Perhaps, though, it is Jesus who acts as the prophet to those who most need to hear.

We listen to the Gospel and to most people, this parable of the dishonest steward is troubling. It appears as if Jesus is rewarding dishonest behavior. It appears that Jesus is holding up as a positive example, this cheating, self-serving steward. And if we look through the lens of the Twenty-first century mentality, indeed it is confusing. But if we put on the sandals of a first century steward, the meaning becomes quite clear.

Jesus doesn't mention where this steward is, but the people of the Ancient Near East understood well the system. The paths that Jesus trod passed through an outpost, what we might call "the boonies." Rich lords had land everywhere, because the land was fertile here; however, there was no city life, and it certainly was not a major polis within the Palestinian world. So these rich lords would entrust the land and products to a steward. The steward would be told the percentage of the profit that was to be sent to the lord and then anything over and above that, the steward could keep for himself. This was how he made his living, on the commission exacted from the customers.

These lords, however, were not dumb and realized that they had a business to run. Word obviously got back to the owner that his steward was not doing "good business" and so he decided to replace him. This is where it gets confusing. The steward was trying to do a little *quid pro quo* in order to ensure his livelihood. He calls in all the customers who have debts with him, because of the exorbitant prices, and begins to reduce the payment. How can he do such a thing? Because, what he is cutting from their debt, is his commission. Again, word gets back to his employer, and yet to his surprise, the employer is delighted, and sees how resourceful he can be...not with the employer's money, but with his own. There is nothing more sobering than an execution... especially if it's your own.

Jesus gives the man credit on two counts. The first is that he did not simply say "Woe is me" and become a burden, so much as he took matters into his own hands and used his gifts to think about the future. Secondly, he's saying it was good that he sacrificed his commission, in order to store up a treasure that cannot be seen or touched; a treasure that is safe from rot or thieves. And that is the message for us. We cannot afford to wait until the last days to prepare for them; that will be too late. We need to use the gifts that have been entrusted to us now, to build up the kingdom of which we will one day reside.

TWENTY-SIXTH SUNDAY IN *TEMPUS PER ANNUM*

AMOS 6:1, 4-7; 1 TIMOTHY 6:11-16; LUKE 16: 19-31 PSALM 146

Facilis descensus Averno; sed ad auras evader est labor![66]

The angels were created instantaneously. Imagine, full infused knowledge and wisdom of all things in the universe, in time and space and beyond. Beings of light, all in the presence of God. Can you imagine, infused knowledge? Perfect understanding of everything at one time. With all of that, we might fall into the temptation of believing it was us. That we were doing this by ourselves. I have no doubt that all of the angels were tempted. Think about it…how could one not be tempted. That all of them looked at the beauty which they were; they looked at all they were given and all they could do and if even only for a brief moment, they were tempted to believe that they were gods. And then they were told their creative-purpose was to serve the creatures. The first temptation.

Free will cannot be harnessed. By its nature it is unshackled by everything but itself. And so a fundamental decision had to be made. Would they serve another with their free will; with all the gifts they were given…or would they serve self? Many, despite the temptation placed before them, chose to serve…others chose otherwise.

As soon as the decision was made, the change was instantaneous.

Those who chose not to serve severed themselves from God; separating themselves from pure light, pure beauty; pure goodness. The change was instantaneous as their bodies were stripped of the light and

---

66 "Going to Hell is easy; it's coming back that's hard." Virgil, *Aeneid*, VI, 126.

the dark grotesque ugliness of the rebellious creature broke forth. The blackest cancer we can see is the fairest of their race. Because they were now without God, they were light-less; beauty-less; good-less. Every creature of this world, ugly as they might seem has some characteristic beauty, because God who is beauty itself has fallen in love with them. But not these creatures. So vast is the separation between them and God, that the void casts a dark ugliness that steals life from anything it touches. Hell is real…and eternal.[67]

Abraham replied, 'My child, remember that you received what was good during your lifetime while Lazarus likewise received what was bad; but now he is comforted here, whereas you are tormented. Moreover, between us and you a great chasm is established to prevent anyone from crossing who might wish to go from our side to yours or from your side to ours.'

These creatures, having been stripped of the light can no longer endure the light; it burns their bodies and yet they are not diminished. It casts light on the ugly darkness which is their *flesh* and drives away the coldness of their wills, now frozen for eternity with their "I will not serve". Unable to endure the light, they flee to the farthest reaches of eternity where light no longer penetrates; the coldest depths of infinity so that the ugliness of their rebellion is hidden even from themselves. And there they remain in their eternal frustration; every moment in timeless eternity re-living the moment they chose their lot….all of them fled; except for one.

Even in this bitter grotesqueness one remains to curse God. This one who was once the **bearer of light**, can no longer stand the illumination, and yet It ignores the cutting blades of light through Its spirit as a final act of defiance. It is not satisfied with simply denying God, but seeks to destroy God. Even the mighty Seraphs were not immune to the temptation of Deity. It approaches the throne as an equal, and yet is dwarfed by the pure light of the Almighty. And in Its defiance It smiles; no longer the luci-fer but the *tempter* and *accuser*. It would spend eternity drawing others into Its dark ugliness by convincing the humans of their own ugliness. It would convince them

---

67 Benedict XVI, Addressing a parish gathering in a northern suburb of Rome.

of the absence of a God; convince them of their own godliness, and when It could not deliver the fulfillment they desired, It would accuse them of Its very own sin. It would try to convince them of the despair that It felt eternally. It smiled, because It saw in Its knowledge the person of Christ; and His seeming failure on a hill in Jerusalem. Then as It looked around the realm of non-time and non-space It saw a vast number, too many to be counted; but It a seraph was not intimidated by these less than It. Not wishing to lower Itself to chill the light of their essence, It *thus departed until an opportune time.*

And so throughout history, darkness continues to conceal the evil of sin. Adam and Eve hid themselves; Sodom and Gomorrah was blanketed in darkness; the Egyptians suffered the plague of darkness; and when Christ died...darkness covered the earth. Make no mistake. "Hell is Real...and eternal." For those who sever themselves from God through an act of Sin, Hell is a reality. In that state of sin, we lose all beauty; all goodness; all grace. And yet, we have an opportunity that Lucifer did not. Or do we believe it?

I charge you before God, who gives life to all things, and before Christ Jesus, to keep the commandment without stain or reproach until the appearance of our Lord Jesus Christ that the blessed and only ruler will make manifest at the proper time, the King of kings and Lord of lords, who alone has immortality, who dwells in unapproachable light.

Satan began as the closest to God...Deemed Lucifer, the **"Light Bearer."** Our Creator has offered us the same grace. Paul says to Timothy that he dwells in unapproachable light, but keep in mind, that the light is only unapproachable, to those who cannot **bear it.**

Twenty-Seventh Sunday in Tempus Per Annum

(Respect Life Sunday)

Hab. 1:2-3; 2:2-4; 2 Tim 1:6-8, 13-14; Luke 17:5-10
Psalm 95

What is the price of a life?

In the time of Habakkuk, there were many gods worshiped by the pagans. One of which was named Moloch, and his counterpart was Astarte. Moloch was the god of war and fire, while Astarte was the goddess of fertility for family and crops. Every year the people offered sacrifices to the gods so that their lives might be good. This was common among the people of the time. If the gods were pleased, living was easy, but if not, the people believed they would suffer plagues, disease, famine, etc.

The god Moloch demanded the same sacrifice every year. The sacrifice was made at this large statue, the stone arms extended as if waiting for the gift and his large mouth gaping wide open. Behind the open mouth, fire burned; the place where the sacrifice would finally rest. The sacrifice was always the same; the sacrifice was an infant. The child would be taken from among the villagers in a type of lottery. It would be offered on that stone altar formed of arms and once killed, the lifeless body was cast through the open mouth into the fire.

This, so that the lives of the people might be easier. We ask, how this could happen? How could people stand by and watch this barbaric act? How many of you would stand up and prevent such an atrocity? How could the people in the crowd of villagers; people who were lawyers, politicians, doctors, teachers, mothers and fathers…how could they stand by and allow this to happen? That is the question… how can we stand by and allow this to happen.

You see, people are still sacrificing infants so that their lives might be easier, but it has changed slightly over the centuries. We no longer call it sacrifice, but a "terminated pregnancy" and we no longer call it an infant but a "placental unit" or "zygote". How could this happen back then? How can it continue today?

Habakkuk cries out: *How long, O LORD? I cry for help but you do not listen! I cry out to you, "Violence!" but you do not intervene. Why do you let me see ruin; why must I look at misery?* We ask "Why do you allow this to happen?" and the Lord responds in an echo to our question: *How long, O People? I cry for help but you do not listen! I cry out to you, "Violence!" but you do not intervene. Why do you let me see ruin; why must I look at misery?* "HOW can YOU allow this to happen?!"

We are called by God to be activists. Imagine those standing in the crowd and doing nothing. They witnessed the atrocity and then return to their normal lives. We cannot do that. And as long as we do nothing, we *are* those people! We come to realize that there are some things God will not do. That although God can ensoul this body He creates, He will not guarantee it will have the opportunity to be born. Some things God will not do, because by doing so, He would remove our free will.

So perhaps, we say, "Well I'm pro-life! I promote the birth"… but that's not enough. So we get the baby born, and then what? This Sunday we celebrate "Respect Life Sunday." We respect life from its conception to its natural end. So we are not finished once the child is born. God has chosen us among millions. He has entrusted us with this soul and wants this soul brought back to Him. How do we do this?

I remember very vividly my granddaddy. I can't recall him ever raising his voice once. He was in charge, no doubt about it, and yet he was respected and had an integrity and honor that was second to none. I recall thinking when I was little that I wanted to be like him. That's the grownup I wanted to be. I'm sure you can recall someone in your life who was that person for you as well. How do children learn what they are supposed to be like when they are grownup? They look at the grownups around them, and that's who they will model their lives after.

The problem is, the grownups (the ones they should be looking up to), are not the people we want our children to emulate. The politicians who are creating laws that are contrary to our Catholic morality. The athletes who...well... cheat; and who do *super-human* feats because they are acting in a drug-enhanced body... Hollywood stars who live such public lives and who do whatever they please... singers, or those who think they are singers, showing us the lifestyle that will seemingly bring them happiness, and yet who go in and out of rehab, relationships and retirement so much no one knows what is going on. These are not the adults we want our children to become.

WE must be that adult we want our children to model their lives after. But this will require someone who puts themselves second to their children and their spouse time and again. What a tragedy when I see fifteen year old girls, walking down the street with the stroller in front of them, taking their child for a walk...when they are still children themselves. Who did they look up to? Even if we don't have our own children, we might be the only adult they encounter on a daily basis who will provide for them a role-model beyond reproach. That will mean putting our wants; our needs; our addictions; our tempers on hold for the greater good of the child. We must be that adult for them, because there's far too much at stake not to be.

It can't stop there either, however. Because if we do become that adult, and entrust our child to other adults who we do NOT want them to become, they will undermine all that we have worked to do. WE must be advocates and activists for life, but that is the life of the child before birth and afterwards. We must be those adults we wish our children to become. We might be the only one they experience every day. Even if we are not the only one, if there are more we can't take the chance. There is just too much at stake.

Twenty-Eighth Sunday in *Tempus Per Annum*

2 Kings 5: 14-17; 2 Timothy 2: 8-13; Luke 17: 11-19 Psalm 98

We have been given the power to loose and bind as well...

The love of the Lord is like the sun. It shines on the good and the evil equally. Or like the rain which falls on the just and unjust. We can't understand it, and we don't want to believe it. It doesn't seem humanly possible and perhaps it isn't *humanly* possible and yet all things are possible for God.

Jesus healed all ten lepers. They were cured on the way and yet he asks: *Were not all ten healed?* Only one returns. Perhaps only the one is considered worthy of healing by "our" standards, and yet all ten were healed. Naamen, the arrogant king of Syria, did not want to follow the prescriptions of God and yet out of desperation he finally follows and is healed. By most standards, he was undeserving, and yet the result was the conversion of a nation.

There is a story of a man, who got a flat tire so he pulled off the road. It just so happened that the place he had stopped was a patch of road that bordered an asylum. Behind the chain link fence surrounding the asylum there was a man peering through the fence watching his every move. The man jacked up the car and pulled out the spare, all the while aware that he was being watched. As he was looking at the man behind the fence and rounding the car, he accidentally kicked the hubcap that was lying there with the lug nuts in it. The lug nuts shot into the grass off the side of the road. The man let out a roar and a litany of words I won't repeat here.

He then glared at the man watching him, as though he were the cause of the incident. He sat there scowling, totally hopeless, when the man behind the fence spoke: "Take a lug from the other three wheels and put them on that one." "What?" The man replied. The man repeated, "Remove a lug from each of the other three wheels and put them on that one...that will get you to your destination." "Brilliant!" The man went around the car and did as he was instructed and it worked. He looked up at the man behind the fence and said: "That was amazing...what are you doing in there?" The man replied, "I AM crazy, but that doesn't make me stupid!"[68]

How often can our perceptions imprison someone in a way that prevents them from becoming anything different.

My father was speaking to my brother-in-laws grandmother, who is Hispanic. He knew she wouldn't understand, but when he asked her if she wanted water, he shouted: "DO YOU WANT WA-TER...WA----TER!" My sister commented, "Dad, she's Hispanic, not deaf!" How often we allow our perceptions to guide our actions around others.

Paul says again: *If we are unfaithful he remains faithful, for He cannot deny himself.* The presence of God is within us by grace of Baptism and therefore when we approach each other, the only possible response is love. God who is all goodness and all knowledge and all power, deemed every soul that is alive, necessary, and so we should respond to that with love. Jesus healed all ten lepers...God cured the skeptical king Naaman. Both were undeserving, let's face it, and yet both of them did not depart unaffected by the miracle. Both were changed.

If we can get beyond our misperceptions and misconceptions, then we can encounter the person of Christ within anyone. And if we can do that, those individuals, who before appeared distant at best; and unlovable at worst, all of a sudden become those we are most drawn to. And when we can experience that....then there will be one less leper in

---

68 Charles Allen Kollar, Solution-Focused Pastoral Counseling: An Effective Short-Term Approach for Getting People Back on Track, (Grand Rapids: Zondervan, 1997), 66-67.

the world; then we will have performed the same miracle as Christ… we will have brought someone back from the dead. It should be noted that the cure for leprosy was discovered in the last century, and a vaccine was developed for the prevention of such a horrible disease. No such vaccine can prevent us from creating lepers, by the things we do, or the love we fail to offer to such as these.

Twenty-Ninth Sunday in Tempus Per Annum

Exodus 17: 8-13; 2 Timothy 3: 14-4:2; Luke 18: 1-8
Psalm 121

What makes a Happy Camper's prayer?

Jack's mother went in to check on him before bed. He looked a bit distressed lying there so she asked what was the matter. "I'm praying for something really hard," He responded. "Well, did God answer your prayer?" He said: "I don't know yet…I'm praying for a snow day."

Much ink has been spilled over the topic of prayer. How do we pray? Why do we pray? What does prayer do in my life? We can walk through any of the major book sellers and see shelves of books on prayer, from Kabala to the "Jesus prayer". Even in the secular world, they call it transcendental meditation or "moments of silent reflection" but what does it really mean to pray. Isn't it interesting, that of all the things Jesus did and said, there is only one thing the apostles actually asked him to "teach us."

Psalm 121 is a brilliant and eloquent treatise on our need to pray. Not so much because of a demand from God, but because of all that God has guaranteed for us. *My help is from the Lord, who made heaven and earth. May he not suffer your foot to slip; may he slumber not who guards you: Indeed he neither slumbers nor sleeps, the guardian of Israel. The Lord is your guardian, your shade; he is beside you at your right hand…He will guard your life…your coming and your going, both now and forever.*

What a wonderful picture of our God. Sounds like the perfect parent, who knows exactly what we need when we need it. The one who wants only the best for us, even when we don't know what the "best for us", is. Therefore, our prayer is not so much a begging for something from a God who is a reluctant giver, as much as it is a conversation of trust and gratitude that we have such a God. This is the message Paul is exhorting us to give. He notes: *to stay with this task whether convenient or inconvenient…constantly teaching and never losing patience.*

So when we pray, God already knows what we need…and what we want. However, sometimes it is not that we aren't praying correctly, or aren't praying enough. Sometimes, it's simply that we are praying for the wrong thing. Imagine that…and yet He still provides what we *need.*

In the last five years I have been a priest, my habit has been to take the eighth grade class camping upon their graduation. I have been camping for quite a few years, so it involves a little more preparation, and meals on a massive level, but other than that, it's pretty cut and dry…well, not always dry. For the last three excursions, the weather had been most cooperative, but this year was different. Many of these students had never been camping, and camping in the rain is not fun, at best and miserable at worst. I told the students that if the weather report showed that it would be pouring rain, that the trip would be cancelled.

I studied the weather reports a week before…days before…two days before, the night before and it showed rain and thunderstorms. I repeatedly asked the morning Mass group to please pray for good weather. When I visited the school, I asked each of the classes to pray that we had good weather; and finally at the closing school Mass the same thing.

The day arrived and the morning was spectacular. There was a beautiful sunrise, and it was warm, but not too humid. I had to smile as I wondered at the generosity of God. We were going to depart at 10:30 am, and I had warned them all what the weather report stated. By ten o'clock, dark clouds began to form. Um…where did my weather modification miracle get to? The students got out of school and grabbed their gear. The ratio was about twenty-one girls and five boys, and I don't mean to be sexist, but I wondered how long many of these ladies were planning to camp. Needless to say, we loaded the van and the bus and were on our way. The whole way I was praying for the rain to clear off, at least long enough for us to pitch our tents.

We were now ten minutes into the trip and the first drops hit the windshield. Now, I'm usually pretty prepared and make a plan "B" and "C" etc. I called a priest friend who lived near the campground in case it was too rainy to pitch tents and he offered the basement of their church (which is really nice). As we continued our trip, the rain pounded on the asphalt and steel, it was just buckets of water. How could this be? I kept praying, "Lord for some of these kids it will be their first time camping...please stop the rain and make it nice for them." The only response was the roar of the drops hitting the window and a low rumble of thunder now and then.

Finally, we arrived at the campground. The rain had slowed to a drizzle. The bus was still with us and we hadn't set up camp yet. The plan had been to hike the waterfall trail and then come back and set up camp and make dinner, but the falls trail would not be safe in the rain, let alone enjoyable. I decided to ask the kids: "What do you want to do? We can set up camp in this drizzle and see how it goes, or we can go to the local church and stay there." The response was unanimous: "SET UP CAMP!" I let out a sigh...*was* there anybody up there? Listening?

We set up the tents,(some with a little help) and the moment the camp was set up, the rain stopped. We had unloaded the vehicles in the rain; put the firewood under the van in the rain; set up tents in the rain, and now the rain subsided and I had twenty-eight students looking in my direction with a gaze that said: "What do we do now?" We decided that we would do the activities that had been planned for tomorrow, today, and the falls trail would come tomorrow.

I wanted to make a fire while the rain was not rushing down, and they wanted to swim in the lake (as if they were not already soaked through.) Since we had planned to hike the falls trail, they had all traveled in their bathing suits, so the suits were wet anyway. The whole group, minus me, went to the lake to swim while I stayed back, made the fire, prayed Evening Prayer and got myself organized. They returned in time to get dinner ready while the adults filled water balloons for our evening activity. Many took showers, while others prepared dinner and still others started carving their marshmallow sticks. Every now and then, a little drizzle would ensue, but never a rain.

We had hotdogs and hamburgers, and the kids did well helping to prepare the food and drinks, while the adults were fooling around with the water balloons. I presumed the balloons would be filled without incident…well, ask adult chaperones to do something. I left one hotdog on for myself. I like them blackened. Finally the kids had finished up and I was ready to eat. I prepared my plate and went to wash my hands. Where was my perfectly blackened hotdog? I was sure I had placed it on a plate and was ready to start doctoring it up, and then I saw it. Someone else was scarfing up my dog. I won't mention who it was here (thanks Ruth) but she was obviously enjoying it, and that was enough for me (not really, but it's all about sacrifice, right?).

Having finished our hearty meal, and a game with water balloon slingshots, by eight o'clock everyone had gathered around the fire for stories and legends, both scary and not so scary. Finally, around eleven o'clock, we celebrated Mass around the fire. Thank goodness, during Mass they didn't notice the raccoon who joined the congregation (how often to animals get to celebrate the Eucharist with us?). Mass was ended and each went to their own tent, while I began my evening vigil. I walked people to the bathroom all night, many of whom stayed around the fire for a bit afterwards.

The next morning they began to crawl to life around five-thirty. They didn't believe me when I said they would be up early. As they rose from their slumber, so did the sun, a brilliant fire in the sky marking the beautiful day that would follow. We had a hearty breakfast and cleaned up the camp. We made our way to the falls trail and had a great hike down the falls and then up again, all the while enjoying the wonderful sunshine and glorious day. We ended the hike and the day by thanking God for a glorious time. Not thanking Him for the good weather, which we prayed for, long and hard. But thanking Him for answering the prayer that we *didn't pray:* that we would have a wonderful time.

That's how good our God is. Even when we pray for the wrong thing…He answers the right prayer again and again.

Thirtieth Sunday in
Tempus Per Annum

Sirach 35:12-18; 2 Tim 4:6-8, 16-18; Luke 18:9-14
Psalm 34

The humble will be exalted.

During one of his international trips, Pope John Paul II was struck with a fever. He continued to follow his agenda for the day and one of the polish nuns caring for him commented: "I am worried about your Holiness." He immediately responded, "I too, am worried about my holiness."

Humility. Paul is in Athens, and surrounded by (as my Grandma would call them) "heatherns" and gives one of his most flawless, rhetorically eloquent arguments for the existence of God. Better than Romans, Corinthians, or any of the other letters… absolutely flawless. And when he finishes waiting for the inevitable applause at the center of philosophical culture and rhetoric the people respond, "Maybe we'll listen to you more later." and they walk away. He had two converts and never went back to Athens again.

Humility. The one prayer, that if you ask the Lord for it, He will answer you. Guaranteed always an answer in the affirmative. Why? Because sometimes it is only through that humiliation that we become humble and come to realize that everything we have comes from God….Everything. Which means, what do we owe God?… everything, because it was never ours to begin with. Paul says in his letter to Timothy: *At my first defense no one appeared on my behalf, but everyone deserted me. May it not be held against them!*

Despite such odds, He continues and realizes that if he does anything good and right and true, it is only because God has given him such a gift. Enter the publican and the Pharisee. Despite what Sirach says about the Lord knowing no favorites, this Pharisee obviously sees himself in a position of superiority. So easy is the trap to fall into.

I was a high school teacher at Pequea Valley and it was the fall, much as it is now. I was working so hard through my classes and at the same time preparing lessons. I recall going to bed around twelve every night and getting up at five in the morning to get to school and get my stuff ready. As would inevitably happen, I got sick. I didn't want to miss a day of school, so I was forcing my way through the week. This one class I had, seemed impossible. They were sophomores, and didn't want to work. It was a basic science class that they had to take, and I don't know where they got this group, but the chemistry was wild. I was fed up with them, trying to assert my domination over them (me just a few years older than they) and they were asserting their rebellious sophomoric attitudes with me.

It was a Friday, I was sick and really didn't want to be there. Now when I taught science, I wrote right on the overhead glass and used that as a blackboard. I would write in marker and then wipe it clean and start again. The class was almost over, but my nose was running and my voice was cracking…I was just sick. And then it happened. I heard this tap on the glass of the overhead below and then…the ink from the marker began to run. MY nose had dripped on the overhead glass! The class let out a unanimous "ewww…..ugh! That's gross," and started laughing. Out of sheer exhaustion and probably delirium, I started laughing too, and immediately a transformation occurred. I saw it happen, like rain coming across the field in summer. They saw my humanity; and in that I was no longer threatening to them…but was like them.

From that point forward the class was different…I was different, and they became my favorite class; one I remember to this day in my daily prayers. Humility allows us to be approachable; it allows others to look through us and see the one who is at our very origin. It is in our humble state that we are fully alive, because only when emptied of ***our self***, can God dwell within us.

Thirty-First Sunday in
Tempus Per Annum

Wisdom 11:22-12:2; 2 Thessalonians 1:11-22;
Luke 19:1-10 Psalm 145

Sometimes to see Christ, it is necessary to go out on a limb.

When God created us, he made an eternal investment. From the moment of our creation, not for a second, has He ceased to contemplate us…not for a millisecond has He forgotten us. "Creation means that God from all eternity has been longing for precisely this unique human being. God's longing at a certain moment was so intense that this particular person came into being, to live a life everlasting."[69]

Seemingly impossible. So you can imagine, if you had the power to create such a creature, and that creature strayed from you, how you would wait with anticipation for when that creature would return. But when that creature returned…having repented of the evil done, you would have a choice…would you divorce yourself from them leaving them alone, reminding them that "they left," and is unable to offer forgiveness? Or…would you embrace the creature, grateful for his return, while ensuring that the creature made amends…and empowering them to become better?

Therefore you rebuke offenders little by little, warn them and remind them of the sins they are committing, that they may abandon their wickedness and believe in you, O LORD! We do not punish for our own benefit, but for that of the child. So too, we must not alienate those who have strayed and wish to return. We welcome them back, with the understanding that they will strive to become better people. But

---

69 Rev. Peter Van Breeman, *Certain as the Dawn*, (New Jersey: Dimension Books, 1980), 43.

that does not release us from responsibility. For many of us will do the essentials...go to Church, pray, etc... but is our house in order for the Lord?

Paul speaks to the Thessalonians, but he would well address this letter to us: *We always pray for you, that our God may make you worthy of his calling and powerfully bring to fulfillment every good purpose and every effort of faith...*

This is the plight of Zacchaeus. Imagine if he had not gone out on a limb. Jesus might have continued through that town. God never would have visited the house of the man, and Zacchaeus would have remained poor...for he never would have given half to the poor and four times what he owed to his victims. But in the midst of this crowd, the one who seems most like a hypocrite and least worthy, hosts the Son of God. And Salvation came to that house. We all seem to have a liking for Zacchaeus. This short, kinda' clumsy guy. Maybe because of his humble conversion; maybe because of his generous transformation... or maybe because we see some of HIM in US. We just haven't gone out on a limb yet.

What if Jesus said to you: "I'm coming to your house today?" I don't know about you, but I'd be getting home to clean my house... in fact, I'd probably rent one! In the ancient world, this (pointing to the heart) was the house...the *domus*. That's where we get the word ab-domen from, meaning "away from the house".

Our Lord speaks to us today as we receive him in the Eucharist. We receive God into our *house*. How clean is the house? Is it the best it can possibly be for our Lord? When we answer that question, then we can begin to understand how God can so easily welcome back a sinner...His eternal investment. Because that sinner, humbled by their mistakes; grateful for such a loving God...That sinner is us. All that is required...like Zachaeus, is for us to go out on a limb.

THIRTY-SECOND SUNDAY IN *TEMPUS PER ANNUM*

2 MACCABEES 7:1-2, 9-14; 2 THESS. 2:16-3; LUKE 20: 27-38 PSALM 17

I know my Master is there...

There is a story of a wife who had recently lost her husband after many, many years of marriage. The woman prayed every night that her husband might somehow contact her, so that she might be assured he was alright. One night, her request was answered as he appeared to her in a dream. She asked of his whereabouts and he said: "I'm in a much better place than I was on earth." She replied: "So you *are* in heaven?" He replied: "I didn't say that... I just said a better place than I was on earth!"

The readings for the last few weeks have been focusing on the end times. The reading from Macabbees, and even the Gospel speaks about the next life, and this is natural as we approach the end of our Liturgical year. The prophets are speaking to us about the world to come. Therefore, it follows with such thought provoking testimonies, that we ask the "What are we living for?"

This is a powerful question to ask, amidst all the suffering in the world; amidst our daily trials in life. We can focus on the desires within us...the longings within us that have never been filled, and if I find within myself a desire which no experience in this world can fulfill, the most probably explanation is that I was not made for this world...but for another. And so we look forward to that "Other" with great hope.

A theologian gives this reflection:

Imagine if you could speak to the baby in the womb before it was born. Having never seen the light of this world, knowing only the confines and comfort and warmth of the womb, the baby would, I suspect be pretty skeptical about the existence of a world beyond that womb. In fact, if we could speak to that child, we might have quite a difficult time convincing the child that the world outside is much bigger and that it would be in their best interest to be born. If the baby *were* conscious, it would have to make a real act of faith, to believe in life after birth. It would have to have a great hope, in order to make that step.[70]

And so it is with us. In the past, the saints called the day of their death, their *dies natalis*, or "birthday." But only one who has hope in something beyond this world… anticipates such a birth.

Think about it. The only way seven brothers ever could have welcomed such suffering is that they had hope in something beyond this world. They did not listen to the music of the world…but they danced. As Paul says: *The God who has loved us and encouraged us gives us hope through grace…* that we might be strengthened toward our birth into eternal life. If we believe in the resurrection, we need not fear… because the promise of the Master is there.

A sick man turned to his doctor, as he was preparing to leave the examination room and said, "Doctor, I am afraid to die. Tell me what lies on the other side." Very quietly, the doctor said, "I don't know." "You don't know? You, a Christian man, do not know what is on the other side?" The doctor was holding the handle of the door; on the other side of which, came a sound of scratching and whining. As he opened the door, a dog sprang into the room and leaped on him with an eager show of gladness. Turning to the patient, the doctor said, "Did you notice my dog? He's never been in this room before. He didn't know what was inside. He knew nothing except that *his master* was here, and

---

70 Adapted from Fr. Ronald Rolheiser. *Against the Infinite Horizon: The Finger of God in Our Everyday Lives.* New York: Crossroad Publishing Company, 2001, 116.

when the door opened, he sprang in without fear. I know little of what is on the other side of death, but I do know one thing... I know *my Master is* there; and that is enough."[71]

Jesus reminds us that those who are deemed worthy of the coming age can no longer die. Because they are born completely; because they have suffered the trials and found the thing that was just beyond reach...and so they are like the angels who dance not for music, as we do....but who dance out of pure joy!

---

71 Internet Forward.

Thirty-Third Sunday in
Tempus Per Annum

Malachi 3: 19-20; 2 Thessalonians 3: 7-12; Luke 21: 5-19   Psalm 98

The world needs heroes...witnesses to the Faith

It was a week away. The priests of the Diocese of Harrisburg were away for our Annual Priests' Workshop, at Hunt Valley, Maryland. It was a great week, and we always enjoy it. If we can take pride in anything, legitimately, we take pride in the priests of the Diocese of Harrisburg. We do have a great presbyterate, and therefore, this week is a great time to be together. We were all dressed casually all week long, not like the normal black shirt and slacks we are accustomed to. We were nearing the last conference, and Fr. Dan had asked me to help him take the left over flowers to his car, so that he could use them in the parish. We were loading the flowers into his car and a drama unfolded.

As we loaded the flowers, we heard a scuffle happening up on the hillside of the hotel, leading down to the parking lot. My first instinct was that there were college students just wrestling or fooling around up there on the hill, but in a moment, that first impression changed drastically. All of a sudden, I heard someone shout, "Stop!" and then I saw a guy running down the hill in a hooded sweatshirt, with a wad of bills in his hand. I don't know what I was thinking at that moment, but all of a sudden, I dropped the flowers and ran... ran after him! I sprinted across the parking lot and soon caught up with him. I grabbed hold of his arms as he was running and said, "Go down!" but he continued to run. I was running out of breath myself, so I gave a final charge and tackled him. We both fell forward and as we landed, I grabbed his arms and put him in a double chicken-wing. I

160

sat there on top of him, happy to hear the footsteps running up behind me as Fr. Mitzel was backing me up. The police followed shortly after with weapons drawn. It was then that I heard over their talkie, that there was an "intended weapon." What did that mean? It meant that this guy had a gun, or at least he said he did.

Money was scattered around us, tipping on its creases with the slight breeze. As the police arrived, I released him, and he sat down and lit up a cigarette as if this was an ordinary "day in the life" (and perhaps it was). Then, the police asked my name for the report. "I'm Fr. Michael Rothan," I said. "Wait a minute…you're a priest? Oh man, we gotta get the news on this!" I was taken in and questioned regarding what had happened and told them what I knew. My adrenaline was still pumping through my veins. Later on that year that I received a citizenship award from the City of Baltimore for apprehending a thief.

The ceremony took about ten minutes, and I showed up dressed as a priest this time. It was a good time for some positive press for the priesthood.

I find it humorous, if not ludicrous, that some people will look on someone who has faith as weak or cowardly. Isn't it interesting, that those who seem so strong in the faith are seen as conformists or individuals unable to think for themselves? They are the ones who back down from a fight. The ones who are supposed to be humble, which is seen as a vice in this world. They are those who are supposed to be lowly in a *dog-eat-dog* existence where "survival of the fittest" is the rule of the day. Where does the faithful Catholic fit into this society? They don't! They exist in opposition to such a society. And let's face it… that society is the majority at this point…and such a minority standing up to a majority does not resemble cowardice or weakness so much as it does heroism.

Don't get me wrong, I'm not saying we have to chase a thief, (in fact, had I thought about it longer, I probably would not have done it either) but we must know who we are, and what we stand for. You see, our Church does not need wusses…it needs heroes. And heroes are not those who can fly or speed around, who ride in invisible jets or fire webs with the flick of a wrist. The heroes are those who are in this world…but not of this world. They are the ones who consistently present themselves as authentic Catholic Christians, convicted by the faith they call their own. These are not those who flee to the mountains, but who *do not worry about their defense beforehand.* They trust that all they need is from God, and they *fear not the one who can kill the body… but the one who can render the soul to Gehenna.*

This gospel message is one to the heroes, who even in their zeal are scared. *You will be delivered up even by your parents, brothers, relatives and friends, and some of you will be put to death.* Um…I'd be a little scared too. But it pushes the issue of whether or not we are ready to be true witnesses, the word from which we get *martyr.* If we complain about the least inconveniences in the faith, what will we do when we're really challenged. That's what I mean by wusses. Do we repeat in our confessions that we ate meat again on Friday because we forgot, having forgotten the fact that we are to abstain from meat on every Friday during the year, unless we substitute it for some act of charity? Are we the ones who complain about Holy Days of Obligation, or try to get a dispensation from Mass while we're on vacation? Do we wear whatever we want to Mass, so that we won't be uncomfortable, or can go on about our day afterwards without having to change clothes? Do we complain because the celebration is not entertaining enough for us, or can't keep our interest? Do we complain because there are children at Mass, making their normal squeaks and squawks? Do we leave right after communion, so we can have the "pole position" when we depart?

The reason you're probably laughing right now is because you know someone like this…right? Because Lord knows *we're* not like this. But really, ask the question: someone who acts in these ways… are they really going to die for the faith, let alone suffer even on a nominal level? No! We do not need more wusses. We need heroes. How do we know when we are heroes? Jesus gives us the indicating factor regarding the world…the world that contradicts us: *All will hate you because of me, yet not a hair of your head will be harmed.* As Fulton Sheen would say: "Search for the religion that is most persecuted by the spirit of the world…and you have found the religion that is divine." The world needs heroes…are you ready to be one?

CHRIST THE KING

2 SAMUEL 5: 1-3; COLOSSIANS 1: 12-20; LUKE 23: 35-43 PSALM 122

Dominion and Domination

Isn't it interesting that Jesus is often called "Lord." We think of this term in a theological sort of way, but think for a moment like someone who does not know God. The term would still have great meaning and import. The Lord, or King was the ruler of peoples. But I would suggest two types of kings; to styles of rule: Dominion and Domination. Having distinguished the two, it should become obvious why we celebrate this feast as the crown of the Liturgical year.

The first reading is from the Second book of Samuel: *Here we are, your bone and your flesh. In days past, when Saul was our king, it was you who led the Israelites out and brought them back.* It takes more than a crown to be a king. It is about relationship. That verse from Second Samuel sounds very much like this one from Genesis: *This at last is bone of my bones, and flesh of my flesh; she shall be called Woman, because she was taken out of Man.* In that statement, Adam is speaking about Eve as much more than simply a companion or helper. He is speaking about relationship. And covenant means *relationship*.

The king who is invested in his people, and who loves them, exercises dominion. Dominion means that he is responsible for caring for those entrusted to his charge. He must make sure they are housed, and fed, and protected. This relationship, however, is not one-sided. The people who live within the dominion of the king agree to help take care of the kingdom, to help defend the kingdom and to pledge obedience to their king. This is how a covenant relationship works. Is it any wonder that after God created man, He also gave him dominion. *Then God said, "Let us make man in our image, after our likeness and let them have dominion over the fish of the sea and over the birds of the air and over the cattle and over all the earth.*" Dominion.

Domination is different. Domination exists where one makes decisions and acts in a way that enthrones the "self." Power is in the service of the ego, as opposed to the service of Love. The dominator uses those around him for his own benefit; makes laws and decrees that serve his interests; and does what is necessary to maintain such a lifestyle. This *Royal Consciousness*, seeks to create in the people a pride for accomplishment; an enslavement of others to build up the kingdom and a silencing of any who oppose.[72] A kingdom of domination necessarily incorporates a Royal Consciousness among its people.

Jesus speaks of a Royal Consciousness when he is among two parties: The Pharisees and Pilate. *The Pharisees lord it over them; but it shall not be so among you. Whichever of you should be the Master, he is the one who will serve the others.* The Pharisees needed to maintain domination, because without their power, they were like everyone else. Pilate shares a dialogue with Jesus about power. For Pilate, power is about the ability to free a man or crucify him; power is about respect and recognition from Rome; power is about control. But for Jesus, true power is always in the service of love. And this is how he closes the dialogue. Is it any wonder why Pilate forced the epitaph on the cross to remain: "This is the King of the Jews."

We see in kingship the two models that have been applied throughout the centuries: Domination and dominion. Adam was given dominion and yet because he clung to that which he had no right to have, he stepped over the line and domination was born. Jesus is now the New Adam, offering a second chance to all who are under his Lordship. He offers them protection; he offers them food; he offers them shelter; and he offers them eternal life. Only one thing remained for the king to do in order to guarantee all these graces to his subject. The only thing that was required, was the sacrifice of his very life. Dominion is the kingship which gives out of pure love, in which absolute power resides. That's why Christ IS King.

---

72 For more on *Royal Consciousness*, see Walter Brueggemann, *The Prophetic Imagination*, (Fortress Press, 1978), Chapter 2.

AFTERWARD

Who was it who said: "An unexamined life is not worth living"? We have so many stories to tell, and yet they never get told. Why? Because we are too busy. People will say, "I'm too busy to pray, or to get away, or to read, or to reflect. Fr. Bill Sullivan once told me: "If you're too busy to pray, then you're too busy." And that was before I was a priest. We all have that need to calm and stop and recollect. Therein is the genius of God…He who needed no rest, rested on the seventh day…to give us an excuse to do the same. We do so many things simply by habit that we don't even think about them anymore. Sometimes that can be good, if they're good habits, and yet sometimes, we become like machines, just going through the motions without finding any meaning in those motions.

I remember going out with my dad to get my Pop Pop (his dad). The police had found him in the middle of the night, in his car, parked in the grass by a store. He didn't know who he was, or where he was; he had a stroke. After days in the hospital it was necessary to take him to a nursing home. He would walk around aimlessly, confused and at times belligerent wanting to do all the things he once did. I decided one day to take him bowling.

My Pop Pop was a sports enthusiast to say the least. Often, he would come over on a Sunday for dinner and watch whatever game was on, from baseball to bowling. He went to a bowling alley in Lancaster and they all knew him there very well. The moment we walked into the place, it lit up. The manager came out and greeted him, amidst others who approached him to ask where he'd been. He didn't recognize any of them. It was so sad to see how their faces dropped when he didn't know them. He walked right over to the lane, picked up his ball and began.

I don't know what I expected really. He didn't know anyone here, so that wasn't helpful to him. And after he threw the first ball down the alley, I got the impression, this whole experience wouldn't do him any good either. He rolled a gutter ball. Second ball, he rolled a gutter ball. And then I saw something different. It looked like his old style… as I remembered it.

He eyed up the pins with the blank stare that had taken over his eyes since the stroke. He walked up and threw the ball, and to my astonishment, strike! Everyone around us clapped. The manager came down and congratulated him. He noticed nothing, but simply stood at the mouth of the ball return, awaiting his bowling ball. The mouth spit it out; he picked it up and threw it down the alley…another strike! Again the people clapped for him, but he continued, unaware of the adulation; he picked up the ball from the track, lined it up and threw it down the alley. Another strike! No one clapped now; now everyone was quiet. Bowlers from nearby began to walk over toward the man who had never had a perfect game. He picked up the ball again… strike! Strike! Strike! He finished out the last frame with three strikes in a row. At this point, he had bowled seven strikes in a row. It was unbelievable. He didn't wait long for the board to clear, he just picked up his ball and started again. Strike! Unbelievable. What I would've done for a video camera. Again, Strike! He would bowl four more, for a total of thirteen strikes in a row. And then he was done. He went and sat down; took off his shoes and put the ball away. I still have the score card. I'll never forget it.

He couldn't remember anything, nor anyone and yet he bowled better than he did when he was aware. Some things become so engrained within our personality, that we don't even notice we're doing them. And yet, he couldn't even enjoy the strikes…because he wasn't aware of what he was doing.

He had a stroke…that explains why. What is our excuse? People will say to me: "how can you be in the woods, all alone?" I guess that would be a valid question…if I were alone. I sit here writing this, and a spider-wasp is right above on the ceiling of the porch, forming a nest for her brood. I hear the chirping of a solitary Vireo, who has made her home underneath the porch, having made her nest on the gas line. A fox squirrel has just tumbled through the woods, like a ball rolling down the hill. A walking stick is deliberately stepping, as if he were passing through a mine field. I hear the distant squawk of a deer who has been disturbed and is putting everyone on high alert, and the scream of a red-tailed hawk soaring over the valley. In the distance, there is a chainsaw, as someone is storing up wood for the winter, and the sound of a lonely owl, asking perpetual questions. None of these creatures will approach me, and even Joey the fawn (so named by my niece) freezes when he sees me, and then darts high-tail into the underbrush. I hear them; I see them, but they are too scared to come close. There is too much to lose. But I am certainly not alone. There is a comfort having them around me. I do not fear them anymore than I would my friends or family.

And yet…I meet people every day who live in the city…or the suburbs, who are surrounded by people everywhere and claim they are alone. How is that possible? Perhaps…no, it couldn't be…perhaps people are afraid. They see others and know they're there; but to get close… to make contact is too dangerous. There's too much to lose. I imagine often times, how alone Jesus must have been. Here he is, the Son of God, amidst people who don't understand. But he wasn't alone as long as he was in communion with the Father. Luke's Gospel is so important because it gives us an excuse to be alone with our God. Not lonely, but alone. He teaches us that to go out to the desert; to go up to the mountain; to go out on the sea; is a necessity in a world that is too busy. But being the Gospel of Women and the Poor, it also teaches us that those who are lonely, are not necessarily in that situation by choice. Sometimes, we are the ones who have made them that way; we are the ones who have no offered them any other option.

Luke shows us in a wonderful way, that we are all called to be the family for the one who has none; to be the friend who is friendless; to be the shelter for the homeless. "Because if I take the time away and look at the story which is my life, instead of just going through the motions, I will come to realize in a very real way, that the one most in need of a Savior; a friend; a shelter…is me."

APPENDIX I
FEAST OF THE IMMACULATE CONCEPTION
(HOMILY OFFERED AT LEBANON CATHOLIC)

GENESIS 3: 9-15, 20; EPHESIANS 1: 3-6, 11-12; LUKE 1: 26-38 PSALM 98

God could have chosen anyone to be the mother of His Son. He could've chosen the mother with thirteen children already; He could've chosen the woman who was sixty years old and had much experience, I mean Sarah was ancient when she gave birth to Isaac (Bet she wasn't laughing then.) He could've chosen the child psychologist, or the professional. Even going a bit younger, he could've chosen the high school junior… but He didn't. He chose an eighth grade girl! What kind of sense does that make! I mean really. Look at this eighth grade girl…(Monica so generously volunteered) she's hyper; likes to talk on the phone or be on the internet or plugged into a machine constantly. Did I mention she's hyper? But He chose her! He created her, when He could have created anybody else.

We know that God is the best of everything. Which means He is also all knowing, all intelligent. Why would he have picked someone so young? Because at that time, it was the youngest age at which one could have a baby. Okay, but why not one a little older? That's a good question…let's see if we can answer it.

Maybe you remember a time in your life when you were so devoted to God. When you might have done things wrong, but you still felt guilty for it; when you prayed every night, and sometimes your prayer would go on and on, because you didn't want to leave anyone out. You went to Church, even if you didn't want to; and when you were there, you would sing and pray and listen, even if the homily was boring. You knew how to pray the rosary, because you did pray the rosary. You knew the Stations of the Cross, and even though you were tired, or hungry or both, you still felt a comfort there. When you really believed at your first Communion that the thing that looked like bread really was Jesus…the greatest treasure.

What happened to those days? Because I know some of you are still living them. When did all that change? When we started to care about what others thought of us, and stopped thinking about the One who matters most. When I was mentioning those things and watching you, some of you had a smile cross your face… because there's a comfort there.

I think that's why God chose someone so young. Because He knew the devotion of someone so young. He knew how the young people could be before the world gets a hold of them. Isn't it interesting that God could have chosen any grown-up…but he chose YOU…he chose a child. That the responsibility of saying "yes" to bringing our Salvation into the world rested on a Junior High Girl! And it still does today.

The Lord is asking the same thing of each of you that he asked of our Blessed Mother. ARE YOU WILLING TO BEAR MY SON TO THE WORLD? It's not too late to rekindle that devotion to our God that you once had. That comfort that formed a smile across your face only moments ago. It's not too late to say YES to God, and thus share with Mary, her great vocation to be the bearer of Christ to the world.

APPENDIX II
ASH WEDNESDAY
(HOMILY OFFERED AT LEBANON CATHOLIC SCHOOL)

JOEL 2: 12-18; 2 CORINTHIANS 5: 20-6:2; MATTHEW 6: 1-6, 16-18 PSALM 51

"Smoke filled the cabin; we thought that the stewardesses had burned something. We were on our way back from what appeared to be a flawless trip. The stewards then began to find volunteers who would help with evacuation of the jet, when we would crash land into the sea. Many were trembling uncontrollably; others crying; one woman writing love letters to her family; we banned together and began to pray."[73]

This is from the paper last week. From an interview of one of the students from Messiah college who was on the plane that almost didn't land.

What is most amazing, is that these college students would turn first, to prayer. Amidst all the professional people, wealthy people, experienced people, and probably even religious people on that plane, only these four began to pray. Too bad it takes suffering or an experience of the desert sometimes to drive us towards this relationship with God. I would like to read to you from a book. This is an excellent book about a woman who became the hunted during the Rwandan holocaust. She was much like many of you. She went to Church because her parents did; went to Catholic school; knew how to pray the rosary and some devotionals, but was not a saint or mystic by any stretch. She prayed as most of you would, at meals or before bed, or before a test. But her relationship with God was also, not something entirely real. Until she entered the bathroom.

---

73 Story paraphrased from the Patriot News, Harrisburg PA

She was hidden in the bathroom of a local pastor. She was scared from what she had already experienced, let alone, what was yet to come. She felt despair, and she writes:

> That's when the devil first whispered in my ear. *Why are you calling on God? Look at all of them out there…hundreds of them looking for you. They are legion, and you are one. You can't possibly survive – you won't survive. They're inside the house, and they're moving through the rooms. They're close, almost here…they're going to find you, rape you, cut you, kill you!*

My heart was pounding. What was this voice? I squeezed my eyes shut as tightly as I could to resist the negative thoughts. I grasped the red and white rosary my father had given me, and silently prayed with all my might: *God, in the Bible you said that You can do anything for anybody. Well, I am one of those anybodies, and I need You to do something for me now. Please, God, blind the killers when they reach the pastor's bedroom – don't let them find the bathroom door, and don't let them see us! You saved Daniel in the lions' den, God, You stopped the lions from ripping him apart… stop these killers from ripping us apart, God! Save us, like You saved Daniel.*[74]

They survived that visit, but as time went on, Immaculae became much more mystical in her prayer. Again, the killers came, and they were getting closer. She continues:

> My scalp was burning, and the ugly whispering slithered in my head again: *Why are you calling on God? Don't you have as much hatred in your heart as the killers do? Aren't you as guilty of hatred as they are? You've wished them dead…*

My thoughts were paralyzed. I knew that the demon in my head was right – I was lying to God every time I prayed to him.…I tried again, praying for Him to forgive the killers, but deep down I couldn't believe that they deserved it at all. *Please open my heart, Lord, and show me how to forgive. I'm not strong enough to squash*

---

74 Immaculae Ilibagiza, *Left To Tell: Discovering God Amidst the Rwandan Holocaust*, (California: Hay House, 2007), 78.

my hatred – they've wronged us all so much…touch my heart Lord, and show me how to forgive.[75]

I drifted off to sleep and shortly before dawn I had a vision of Jesus in front of me and he spoke. "When you leave this room, you will find that almost everyone you know and love is dead and gone," he said. "I am here to tell you not to fear. You will not be alone – I will be with you. I will be your family. Be at peace and trust in me for I will always be at your side."[76]

It's a terribly wonderful book; a fantastic story about a terrible tragedy. But a wonderful story because it is the story of a relationship with God. This is what Catholic education is all about. This Mass, is the most important thing we do here. The retreats, reconciliation, the prayer services are the most important things we do here. Why? Because no other school can give you the tools to develop a relationship with God. No other school can empower you with such things to face the crises in life.

When Immaculee was in the bathroom and the killers were outside, she didn't turn to her scientific knowledge, or her literature or her French. She didn't try to recall trig. identities or even the Vatican II documents. She recalled the prayers she had memorized; she prayed the rosary and read scripture. She reverted back to all she learned about a relationship with God. All the things you learn here are necessary for life; but the most important one, is that one which will bring you closer to eternal life.

The students on the plane prayed. These are the deserts we will deal with in life. I have been to the hospitals with people dying of some earthly disease, who have no faith. They want YOU to give them something they don't have. Take this Lent to *rend your hearts and not your garments* as the prophet says. To rend garments is easy…but our hearts?! To do something superficial like give up candy or something visible is much easier than surrendering the thing we want least to give up. I challenge you to enter the desert through this Lent. For forty

---

75 Ibid., 92-93.
76 Ibid., 111 – 12.

days, you will be chaste; you will be sober; you will give up the drugs that cloud reality; you will not gossip; you will surrender your grudge against your former friend; you will befriend the one who has no one. Suffer a little, and work on your relationship with God.

I know sometimes religion class can be difficult; I know there's a lot to know and memorize and all of it is important. But what is most important, and what I want most for you now, is to develop a personal relationship with the One who created you. Because if you don't have that…then the rest will one day prove useless.

APPENDIX III
HOMILY FOR HOLY THURSDAY
MASS OF THE LORD'S SUPPER

EXODUS 12:1-8, 11-14; 1 CORINTHIANS 11: 23-26; JOHN 13: 1-15 PSALM 116

The gospel story from John this evening is one that is told every Holy Thursday. You've heard it many times, and yet, tonight I want to focus on the import of this passage for our journey. This evening, there are two who would encounter Christ in a way that was different from all the others. Two, who would be looked in the eye by their Lord at a time which was critical for them. These two were Peter and Judas.

Again, we must go back to the Greek words or risk missing something of what Christ was saying. Don't you find it strange that after Christ explains why he must wash him, all of a sudden Peter is all into it? The fact is, there are two different words for wash used here in the original text. When we see the difference, the passage is a powerful message on what it means to tend the sheep. The two words for wash are *nipso* vs. *leloumenos*.

The word *nipso* in Greek, means simply to wash. It is what we do with dishes or a body, we wash it. The word *leloumenos* was a military term. It meant "to wash out the mortal wounds that a soldier suffered in battle." If we put those words into the Gospel from John tonight, it sends a powerful message to all of us.

Peter says: *You will never wash me* (nipso)." Jesus says, *Unless I wash you* (leloumenos *or unless I wash away your mortal wounds) you have no inheritance with me.* Then Peter wants not only his feet washed, but his whole body. Peter has given up everything to follow Jesus; he now accepts the reconciliation that he will require again later on, but he accepts it now. Jesus looks at him and loves him.

What about Judas? Imagine looking up at the one you know is about to betray you…eating dinner with him…washing his feet. The one who will betray you! And even then, Jesus was giving him another chance. Another chance to start over. Judas approaches Jesus in the garden and addresses him "Rabbi". He might as well have said "Mister." Jesus replies "friend" but the Greek word used, *etaure*, means my most intimate friend. In the Septuagint, David uses this word for Jonathan. Jesus looks at him…and loves him. We will never understand the drama that unfolded as these sweet words carried their virulent message to the ears of Christ. For in the ancient world, to listen was to make the words a part of the self. Someone who was his most intimate friend signed the warrant for his death.

This responsibility we have, as a result of the great gift that Jesus has given us, is our commitment. The gift of himself in the Eucharist is something we could never afford, and can never repay. It is the ransom paid for a death sentence. All he asks in return is the same thing he asked of Peter… "Be washed"; and of Judas… "Be my most intimate friend".

APPENDIX IV
GOOD FRIDAY HOMILY
THE SEVEN LAST WORDS

ISAIAH 52: 13-53; HEBREWS 4: 14-16; 5: 7-9; JOHN 18: 1-19, 42 PSALM 31

"Seneca wrote: 'Those who were crucified cursed the day of their birth; the executioners, their mothers; and even spat on those who looked upon them... Cicero recorded at times say that sometimes it was necessary to remove the tongues of those crucified because of their terrible blasphemies.[77]   The scribes and Pharisees awaited his reaction and they were quite sure he who had preached "Love your enemies" and "Do good to those who hate you", would now forget the Gospel with the piercing of his body. Weren't *they* surprised?...Not so with the Christ. From his cross he spoke seven last words...all words of love.

Like a fragrance that trees bathe in perfume the very axe that cuts them down, his first words were those of forgiveness: *Father forgive them*...forgive them of their ignorance...but woe to those who know better.

Of all those who could escort the Son of Man into paradise...he chose a thief. *Lord, remember me when you come into your kingdom.* It was the thief's last prayer, and perhaps even his first.   Had Barabbas come to the execution, how he would have wished that he had never been released, so that these words might have been spoken to him.

He addresses his mother; no longer his mother, but *Hevah*: Eve, the *Mother of all creation*. From the moment he addressed her at the wedding feast in Cana in the same word, his "hour" had begun. And now at its completion once again he looks to her. Back then, he had made it clear that the world could not tolerate his divinity; so that as he turned water

---

77 Bishop Fulton Sheen, *Life of Christ*, (New York: Image Books, 1977), 372.

into wine, he would one day change wine into his very blood. At the cross, this was a second annunciation; as Mary is told she will be mother of the world. And again, without hesitation, she gives her *fiat*.

Nature mourned with its Creator, so that even as the world was destroying the *light of the world*, the sun became darkened. And in becoming sin, he who knew no sin, also felt the darkness. Just as a cloud passes over the sun for just a moment, darkening the landscape, so too does Jesus feel total abandonment as he takes on the clouds of sin and cries out in a loud voice.

Finally he directs a word on his own behalf.... "I thirst." When he was crucified he refused to take a drink that would dull the pain and his senses. Now he asks for a drink. He who had turned water into wine at Cana could have done the same here except for the fact that he would never perform a miracle for himself.

"It is finished." His life from the time of his birth to the time of his death had faithfully achieved all that the heavenly Father sent him to do. Three times God used the *word* in history: the first at creation, the second in the apocalypse, and here, spoken from the lips of Christ, at the highpoint in history of salvation. All of the Old Testament prophecies are fulfilled in him.

Finally he addresses the Father, offering his spirit. "His sixth word was earthward; the seventh Godward."[78] It is difficult for someone who thinks of dying as the most terrible crisis and failure of life, to understand the joy that inspired these words of the dying Christ. "The peril of living is greater than the peril of dying."[79] As these words were spoken, there came from the opposite hill of Jerusalem the sound of thousands of lambs who were being slain in the outer court of the temple that their blood might be offered before the Lord God on the altar, and their flesh might be eaten by the people.

"In the last moments, there was a rupture of a heart in a rapture of love; the Son of Man bowed His head and willed to die."[80]

---

78 Ibid., 385.
79 Ibid., 386.
80 Ibid., 387.

APPENDIX V
ASCENSION OF OUR LORD

ACTS 1: 1-11; EPHESIANS 1: 17-23; LUKE 24: 46-53
PSALM 47

To Inspire and Empower

Imagine for a moment losing someone twice. In this age of advancement in medical technology, it is not uncommon to bring back those who were considered "dead" at least on the operating table, or in the ambulance. What could be worse than losing someone? Losing them twice. Imagine a loved one who was considered "dead" and was brought back, only to die weeks, months even years later. How tragic would that be? To actually mourn a death, only to have to mourn again.

Such was the case with the Apostles and their Lord. Jesus has risen! Alleluia! We have seen him. He has appeared to us at the tomb, on the road to Emmaus; in the upper room; on the sea; and in Galilee. *Lord, are you going to restore the rule of Israel now?* They said. They probably thought: "We mourned his crucifixion and death, but now he is back with us. And now"…he must leave us. Jesus prophesied all the wonderful things to come, and so they were filled with joy…and then he was gone.

At this point, I imagine Peter was the first to speak up and say: "Now what?" They stood there for a bit, as often people will do with the last breath of a loved one, waiting in anticipation to see if they will breathe again. They waited to see him coming on the clouds for their immediate redemption, but they were left in anticipation. And then two men appeared dressed in white. This was it! The moment they were waiting for. Surely, Jesus was returning and all would be well; one would sit at his right and the other at his left. And the two spoke: *Men of Galilee, why do you stand here looking up at the skies? This Jesus will return...* and then... "Get up and move people! You gotta start a Church!"

I remember one of my first pastoral experiences. I was so nervous, that I prayed for an hour before. I knew this was going to be a difficult counseling situation, but was reassured because the pastor would be present. I asked him to be there in case I got "stuck" or something happened. I reviewed, very carefully, all the steps I should use in this situation and was ready for anything. The couple arrived for counseling, and we sat there awkwardly looking at each other. I knew them vaguely, just from being in church, but the Pastor had some experience with them. We waited, staring awkwardly at each other.

Where was he? I excused myself as I left the office and wanted to be *anywhere* but there at that moment. I wandered around aimlessly, trying to figure out what to do; surely he would come, just a little late. I went back into the room, and they looked irritable. They were not speaking to each other, and both were nervously looking at their watches. And then the Holy Spirit moved me: "Why don't we get started, and I'm sure the pastor will be along shortly." He never came.

He never showed, but we had the session... and it was an absolute disaster. I had control for about the first thirty seconds, and even that is debatable. One started to accuse the other, while the other retorted, bringing up past wounds. All the rules, all the methods I had so carefully memorized went out the window. I sat there helpless to do anything. Was this going to be the priesthood for me? Fifty-plus years of this?!

Finally it was getting close to the hour, and they both stopped talking. They looked at me as if I were some highly paid counselor or guru and would immediately provide an answer to everything based on the bantering that went back and forth. I was sweating and had a shaky feeling in my stomach. What could I say? I had to do something; so I did the only *thing*, that I *could* do. I began to tell them what I heard them say to each other. I repeated in paraphrase, what she said, and then his responses, more or less. They didn't interrupt, but just sat there, almost as if they had never heard these words before. In a few moments, I was done. I felt like saying "Please return your tray tables

and put your seats in the upright position. Thank you for flying..."
When I finished, they thanked me and left. That was it!

Jesus could have stayed with the apostles forever, and they probably never would have done any more than they did up to this point. There's something to be said for throwing a child in the water to teach them how to swim. Jesus was not willing to let them flounder, by any means, but needed to empower them to become the Apostles who would carry on the work that he began. It was the difference between enabling and empowering. When we enable someone, we give them what they need at that moment, in order to keep them where they are; to empower someone, however, means to give them the ability to move forward, despite the hardship or suffering that might entail. "Give a man a fish you feed him for a day... teach him to fish and he'll never go hungry."[81] Jesus not only inspired the Apostles, but he empowered them, so that they would be able to continue his work, even if it meant one day they would suffer for the *Name*. He not only inspires us, but wishes to empower us, so that we will go forward and draw others close to him through our teaching.

I ran into the pastor later that night, and he was humbled. He told me that he had totally forgotten the whole meeting. Yet, even today, I meet with that couple now and then, already seven years later. And every time we meet, they remind me of how I did so much that night to help save their marriage. I know better. I didn't do too much that night at all, but just as he wouldn't leave them orphans...he didn't leave me an orphan either.

---

81 Lao Tzu. 6th Century BC. Father of Taoism.

APPENDIX VI
HOMILIES GIVEN AT TRINITY HIGH SCHOOL, CAMP HILL PA
-1-

OPENING SCHOOL MASS TRINITY HIGH SCHOOL (ENCOUNTERING CHRIST)

ACTS 9:1-8; MT 19:16-26

This year our theme at Trinity High School is "Encountering Christ." The last two years, we have focused on respect, which means to "look at again" and last year authenticity, which means to "be the person God created us to be." Those two themes, although good, could be found in any school. Although the most important, our theme this year will not be found in a public school, or even a non-Christian private school. And yet, it is the most important thing. What does it mean to encounter Christ and how can we do this?

We have two models today of how this works out. In the first reading, we see this guy Saul, who was a killer of Christians and yet observant in the Law to a fault. The second model is "the rich young man." Here's a guy who has it all, and also follows the Law almost to a fault. Of these two candidates, if you had your vote, which do you think had the better chance of a conversion? Most would probably say the "rich young man". I mean, let's face it, Saul is a murderer of Christians; a rich young man, won't hurt anyone. How does it play out then?

First here comes Saul riding along (now scripture never says he was riding a horse, but it adds to the drama.) Here comes Saul riding along and all of a sudden BOOM. He's knocked off his horse. And the voice says: "Saul why are you persecuting me?" This is fantastic, because the

Greek word here, *dioko* means "follow after in pursuit" to cause fleeing. In other words, Jesus is saying: "Saul why are you following me in this way, as opposed to the way you should." Saul was *blinded*...up to this point he had surrendered everything he had to pursue Christ....but in the wrong way; now finally with his sight taken, he was ready to follow, having encountered Christ.

Second, here comes the rich young man. He has it all...looks, talent, *bling*...even theme music...he has it all, and yet, he too, is pursuing Jesus. He is looking for "life." There are two words that could be used. The first, *bios,* means life, like a flower is living or an insect is living. That is not the word used here. The word this young man uses is *zoë*. This means full rich divine and human life. This is the fullness of life. But isn't this a rich guy? Doesn't he have everything? I mean he's following the commandments and has everything....except the only thing that matters....true full Life. Life which we cannot secure for ourselves. We can only secure it having had an encounter with Christ, and allowing that encounter with Christ to change us forever.

That's what we're talking about here. There are two ways in which we will encounter Christ. The first is when we encounter Him in himself, in the Eucharist, in his word, in our prayer with his presence. The other way we encounter him is through others. We look in others and see Christ, and we ourselves encounter others and show them Christ. This is what it's all about. This is the missing part. Paul was pursuing, but he didn't know why; the rich young man is missing something, but he can't figure out what. Both seek the same thing; both encounter Christ; one walks away while the other becomes the greatest apostle and writer in Church history.

Pascal said: "There are only two classes of men who can be called rational...those who serve God with all their hearts because they know Him; and those who seek Him with all their heart because they know Him not."[82] So what did Saul not have that allowed him to turn and

---

82 Pascal, "Pascal's Pensees 'Apology'", in *The Priest is not His Own*, Bishop Fulton Sheen, (New York: McGraw- Hill, 2005), 90.

follow; and what did the rich young man **have** that kept him away? Attachment.

Attachment typically manifests itself in two ways. First we have an attachment to things. We have so many things in our life. If you doubt this, how many of you needed the "chocolate" the day it came out, even though your old phone worked fine? How many stopped their cell phone plan and got an i-phone the day it came out? How many hours do we spend in front of the computer, video games, or TV; these boxes which have no life, no love, no personality? Yet we allow them to control so much of our time, distracting us from the things that really matter. These things eat up our time, so that we have nothing left.

But another attachment we can have is to people. Not good friendships, that's not what I mean. I'm talking about when we allow others to control who we are and what we do by what they say to us. How we can allow their approval of us to dictate who we are? We can do this to such an extent that we lose who we are.

I challenge all of you to take this year to let go of your attachments. To let go of all those things which draw us away from what is most important. If we can do that, perhaps this year in encountering us, those around us will encounter Christ; and having been freed of those things, perhaps we might also encounter Christ in a way that before we might have considered impossible. *Saul, why are you chasing after me. Who are you Lord? I am the one you are chasing after.*

-2-

TRINITY HIGH SCHOOL: FEAST OF ST. IGNATIUS OF ANTIOCH

PHILIPPIANS 3: 17-4:1; JOHN 12: 24-26

Be imitators of me my brothers. Take as your guide those who follow the example that we set. Unfortunately, many go about it in a way which shows them to be enemies of the cross of Christ... Their only god is their belly and their glory is in their shame. The commandments were only written for those who need them. But many, although they will observe some of the commandments without fail, grievously violate the others. These words are for us. How? I would like to read a few lines from a song I heard at one of our dances. See if you recognize them.

Black Eyed Peas "My Humps" from album: *Monkey Business*, (Interscope Records, 2005).

What you gon' do with all that junk?
All that junk inside your trunk?

I'ma get, get, get, get, you drunk,
Get you love drunk off my hump.

My hump, my hump, my hump, my hump, my hump,
My hump, my hump, my hump, my lovely little lumps (Check it out)

Aside of the fact that this is bad English, and the words are mispronounced, what is the message? Now, I know *you know* this song by the very fact that you started to laugh (probably uncomfortably), and yet I know the excuse I've heard over and over again: "We just like the beat, we don't listen the lyrics." Why then, were some of you mouthing

185

the lyrics along with me? So much so, that when I skipped, you kept going with the proper lyrics. Despite the fact that the lyrics violate all sorts of grammatical precepts, they also *violate the person*…they also commit the gravest of sins…they turn a person into an object.…they reduce a person to sexual parts. Jesus says in John's Gospel: *If anyone would serve me, let him follow me; where I am, there will my servant be. Anyone who serves me, the Father will honor.* Jesus always saw the Father in those he encountered. He would never have reduced a person to an object.

I wonder how many of us would prefer eating out of a dumpster when there is a lavish banquet from which to eat. And yet, we will often settle for the dumpster. We see the women in these videos and on magazines; we see these men like meat plastered over signs and television, and the only thought that comes to mind comes from the mouth of a bishop "How tragic…that such beauty is being sold to the lust of men."[83] We act as if this is the only possible way to respond to each other. That there is no higher purpose than animal sex between individuals. That is the most successful lie our world has propagated.

I see in front of me beautiful, beautiful people. That in your very bodies, God has carved His plan; a plan of man and woman united in a bond so powerful, that they are given the power to share in God's creative act. That man's body by itself doesn't make sense. And woman's body by itself doesn't make sense. It is only together that we see the fulfillment of God's plan. Yet we have eaten from the dumpster for so long, that this sexual union is no longer special. It has become an accessory to a relationship. People say, "Why can't we have sex before marriage?" The fact is you can. But realize, everything we do symbolizes some truth. "When you have sex before marriage, then you know one true thing about each other. You know that you are both willing to have sex with someone you're not married to."[84] And if you can do that now…what would stop you from doing it after marriage.

---

83 Christopher West, *Theology of the Body Explained*, (Pauline Books and Media, 2007), 170.
84 Ibid., Talk given at Priests' Continuing Education Workshop, Hunt Valley MD, 2008.

If you are not committed to purity for your future spouse now, then you are training yourself for infidelity later.

If we have been eating from the dumpster; if we are contaminated; we might say "we didn't know" or "we don't believe that though." Let me ask you this. If someone drinks poison, and they don't know it's poison, are they committing suicide? No. Because they don't know.... but will it still kill them? Absolutely. If you're about to drink poison, and someone stops you.....literally saves your life, how would you respond to that person? With absolute gratitude. Someone who truly loves you...and does not want to see you eat from trash. See, whether we believe this or not, the poison will kill us. When we engage in an act that is supposed to occur only within a sacrament, we profane what is holy, and we suffer because of that.

So, what can we do? If you're with someone now, the two of you together, must begin to *de-tox*. You're too good for that. Imagine how much better it can be, and I know that's difficult because you've not tasted that before. Talk with the one that you love about why not to engage in an act proper only to a lifelong commitment. Pledge yourselves to your future spouse...even if that spouse is the Church! Especially if that spouse is the Church.

And don't listen to the music that hates you. For all of you girls who have ever been abused by a man, this song is an affront to you. To any of you guys who have ever been used simply as an object, this song mocks you. To any of you who have ever been spoken to or treated as though you were simply a body, easy to replace with any face: this song speaks of uselessness as a person, and cheapens your beauty inside and out. To any of you, who have ever felt used and discarded; betrayed; naked; this type of music exalts in your misery. WE don't listen to the lyrics, but like water tainted with a tasteless poison, it slowly infects us. And if we buy the songs of those who propagate such poison, then we are as bad as the lyrics they speak.

-3-

Trinity High School: Ascension Thursday

Acts 1: 1-11; Ephesians 1: 17-23; Luke 24: 46-53 Psalm 47

What if today were your last day? Happens to me sometimes where people will approach and say: "Father...the doctor gives me three weeks." What if today were your last day? You've lived for what seems like a short moment, and then (I had the lights "outed" at this point to darkness) darkness....night forever. That is (lights were then faded up again) unless you believe in something more. And if in fact you do believe in something more; then the fact that today is your last day wouldn't matter; unless you were living for "this" life. "He wanted to stay...but he had to go."[85]

Did you feel the icy cold of the dark? Did you feel alone... unsettled? For some, that is real; for some, that's all there is. Why would anyone want to live for tomorrow, if that's ultimately what we have to look forward to? For this reason, the Ascension is so important to us! Because it proves to us that there is so much more.

I want you to imagine for a minute...really imagine: This IS your last day. Did you do all you wanted to? Make all the money you wanted to? Bought all you wanted? Loved all you wanted? Experienced all you wanted? No?... NO! You cannot possibly, even if you were to live a thousand years. Because we were not made for this world, but for the next. We can't do all we want to do? Buy all we want, experience everything...but love...can we die today saying we loved all we could? Could we leave this world behind this day, knowing that we were good?

---

85 Bishop Nicholas Dattilo. Homily given for the Ascension of our Lord.

I'm not talking good, being good, etc. I'm talking about goodness; would our Creator know our voice, our face, our effect in the world?

My dear friends, we don't have to believe in God in order for Him to exist, anymore than we don't have to believe in bacteria, in order to die of pneumonia. We can deny we have a relationship with Him, but that IS our relationship with Him. We can pretend that this world IS, all there is; but the play must end sometime. You see, to live for God... to live for the next life, does not mean that we forget this one; it does not mean that we deny the real things happening now and the impact of those things... not at all. What it means is that we are IN the world, but not OF the world. It means that we are detached from the "things" in this life in such a way that our happiness does not depend on them; THAT is freedom; anything else is simply an illusion.

How do we obtain this "detachment?" Christ showed us how, but it must be real...not just pretty words; not *sky language*. It means a different existence, where our happiness is no more dependent on things which will never be enough; our peace is not dependent on what people say about us, so much as who we ARE. That we live for the only One who can satisfy our longing.

This is our last Mass with our Seniors. And I imagine, if they could have an Interview with God, it would go something like this:

> I dreamed I had an interview with God. "So you would like to interview me?" God asked "If you have the time" I said. God smiled "My time is eternity."
>
> "What questions do you have in mind for me?"
>
> "What surprises you most about humankind?..."
>
> God answered...
> "That they get bored with childhood. They rush to grow up and then long to be children again."
> "That they lose their health to make money and then lose their money to restore their health."
> "That by thinking anxiously about the future, they forget the present, such that they live in neither the present nor the future."

"That they live as if they will never die, and die as if they had never lived."

God's hand took mine and we were silent for awhile
And then I asked..."As a parent, what are some of life's lessons you want your children to learn?"God replied with a smile:

"To learn they cannot make anyone love them. What they can do is let themselves be loved."
"To learn that it is not good to compare themselves to others."
"To learn that a rich person is not one who has the most, but is one who needs the least."
"To learn that it only takes a few seconds to open profound wounds in persons we love,
and it takes many years to heal them."
"To learn to forgive by practicing forgiveness."
"To learn that there are persons who love them dearly, but simply do not know how to express or show their feelings."
"To learn that two people can look at the same thing and see it differently."
"To learn that it is not always enough that they be forgiven by others. But that they must
forgive themselves."

"And to learn that I am here always."[86]

Imagine this were your last day. But imagine a last day, having lived for the one to whom you were returning; imagine a last day when you can have honestly said, you loved...I mean really loved. Imagine a last day where you were detached from the things of this world in a way that you were truly free. A last day (which can come at any moment) for such a person would not nearly be considered a failure, as the world would have us believe...a moment...and then forever night... NO... such a day; for such a person; we would call, an Ascension!

---

86 Internet Forward

APPENDIX VII
HOMILIES GIVEN AT LEBANON
CATHOLIC HIGH SCHOOL, LEBANON PA

-1-

Lebanon Catholic: Catholic Schools Week

I want you to close your eyes….close them tight. Now, raise your hands. Say "hello." Say it loud! Say your name. Say "I love you." Say it again. Say it again. Now…think of someone you truly love; and say it again. Say "Amen!" Say "Amen!" Why am I doing this? Because. Now…keep your eyes closed.

I want you to remember when you were five, or your earliest age. Think of how funny you looked or how cute you were. Your biggest concern was whether or not today was the day you would actually find the toilet before it found you. Today was a day full of adventure. When you were in daycare, or at home, if you wanted to play, you just went over to a kid and played; play-dough was good…not only to eat, but to play with. Cereal was the best thing; especially if it had those dry-eraser flavored marshmallows or some kind of color. Your biggest concern was whether or not you would have to take a nap. You didn't care what you wore…obviously, based on your outfits…even if you were a "Gap Kid" or a child of a Baby Boomer parent. Your hair was…. well, it covered your head. Life was good…you were loved. What happened? And don't you dare tell me you grew up!

My real question is more specific (keep your eyes closed). When did you start to worry about what others thought? When did you begin to question your worth? Who told you that you grew up? Now before you fall asleep, look at me and listen to this letter to the Hebrews. But this letter isn't only for them…it is for you. A reading from the Letter to the students at Lebanon Catholic

Remember the days past when, after you had been enlightened, you endured a great contest of suffering. At times you were publicly exposed to abuse and affliction; at other times you associated yourselves with those so treated… knowing that you had a better and lasting possession. In other words, it didn't matter what others thought, because you experienced the love of God. *Therefore, do not throw away your confidence; it will have great recompense. You need endurance to do the will of God and receive what He has promised.*

Our Catholic Faith is something to be proud of. If you were a friend of a superstar, a Hollywood model, or a singer, you would proclaim it to the rooftops. But because our love is conditional, we stay quiet when we are among those who do not believe.

How many of you play sports? How many of you are involved in the plays, the band or other activities? When people come to observe you, which ones do you value the most: the ones who got all dressed up to be seen, and really don't watch the event, so much as they socialize; or the ones who cheer or listen attentively and enjoy the show? The one who participates! So why are we not *that one*? Because we're scared. Scared of what? Who has more fun at the dances, the ones who stand along the wall or sit in chairs, or the ones who are on the floor? Of course, the ones dancing, and many of them don't know how to dance, let's face it. They're going from the robot, to fireworks, shopping cart, to MC Hammer! They don't know….but they're having fun, and it doesn't matter. If these things, which are not so important, we do bravely; why is it we cannot bravely practice what is most important?

I know sometimes you probably get grief for your uniforms (I know you give it) and yet I see in those kilts something more than an oppressive uniform. I see a tartan…a tribal symbol which says, we are a clan, a family whose roots reach farther back than this country. How many schools can claim that? I know you probably dread coming in here some days; in fact some might even use the word hate, strong though it may be. I know wherever I go, I proudly announce that I am the chaplain at Lebanon Catholic; so much love do I have for the people here. And yet, without people, this is just a building.

Jesus speaks to us of the mustard seed. The smallest of all the seeds, and yet, when we take it and nurture it, it becomes much bigger than we are. We affect people in a way that might otherwise be impossible. That is what it means to be in a Catholic School; that is what it means to be Catholic. You know it's possible to feel this way, because many of you have had that experience. Do not be afraid!

For, after just a brief moment, he who is to come shall come; he shall not delay. But my just one shall live by faith, and if he draws back I take no pleasure in him. We are not among those who draw back and perish... but among those who have faith and will possess life. We will not be silenced by those who seek to destroy God, but we will be the voice in the wilderness crying out with joy, *These things the Lord has done.*

Today is a new day for bravery. Today is a new day to live your faith as you never have before...to live it bravely for the sake of those whose blood was spilled in days past. And if you waver...if you fear for a moment, relive the words of our great pope John Paul II: (I spoke them in a polish accent) "Be not afraid....be not afraid."

-2-

FEAST OF ST. BLAISE, BISHOP AND MARTYR
LEBANON CATHOLIC (HIGH SCHOOL STUDENTS)

Today we celebrate the memorial of St. Blaise, Bishop and Martyr. He is the patron saint of sickness, especially those of the throat, so it is probably good this celebration is in the winter months, because many of us are already sick, or will probably pick up something soon. After the homily, we will bless your throats through his intercession, which is a powerful prayer.

Certainly our faith in healing is based on the ministry of Jesus, and how he went about all over the land to heal those in most need. In today's Gospel, there are two that are healed. The first is a woman who has hemorrhaged for many years and pretty much used up all of her resources. She had been through doctors, and her friends probably got tired of her complaining or inability to be with them, so she is alone. And yet in all her misery, she realizes the only one who can help her is Christ. But it didn't stop there…she approached Him. She did not put it off, or wait for him to come to her, she initiated the contact, and the cure was immediate.

The official, Jairus comes to Jesus regarding his daughter. How many parents approach Jesus about their children? Even though he's a pagan, Jesus goes with him, but it took the man to speak for his daughter first. Both of these people went to Jesus for healing and he granted that faithful request. Both people suffered from a disease that was within; but sometimes the most dangerous things are not within; they are from the outside. And we put them into our bodies.

For these diseases, Jesus has little power to heal; the intercession of St. Blaise can do little, because of these diseases, we don't want to be healed. But that's not the only problem. Those who have the disease will not be led to Christ by their friends. That is the sad part. Let me give you an illustration and perhaps it will help to clarify my point. I have chosen a volunteer to help out with the homily today. This is her first time here on the stage, and her name is Sadie. (Dog)

[At this point a puppy was brought up front. I took incense and placed it in a metal dish and it began to smoke. I then brought the dog over and threatened to push its face into the smoke. I then took a bowl of ethyl alcohol and told the kids I would led the puppy drink this and see how it acts, or reacts. Finally, I had pills of various sorts and threatened to feed the pills to the puppy, and again see what happens. As I was threatening to do all of these things, you could hear the gasps from the students in the congregation, and the cries advocating for the puppy. And then the second part of the homily commenced.]

Leaves…alcohol…pills…How many of you thought it would be barbaric, if not abusive to do those things to Sadie? Well, if you think this is barbaric or unfair or cruel to do such things to a puppy, then you must love this animal more than you do your siblings or friends. Because if you haven't introduced your friends or siblings to smoking, or drinking, or drugs, then perhaps you at least allow it to happen. We say "I support my friends" or "I'll never betray them or turn them in" or "There were parents at the party, so it was okay" etc. etc. If we say that, then we egregiously misunderstand *support*. Support does not mean to encourage those we love in behaviors that can be deadly to them, or dangerous for others. Support means being the *official* who brings them to Christ for healing; support means not enabling one who is harming themselves to continue.

You know, sometimes Jesus cannot heal. And this blessing through the intercession of St. Blaise will do little to heal the poisons we allow to enter our bodies and those of our friends. We would never subject this animal to the smoke…to the drugs…to the alcohol, because that is cruel. So we must love this animal more than our friends…because if we are not encouraging them in these behaviors, we are at least allowing them to happen. And "in order for evil to occur, all that is necessary is for good people to do nothing."[87]

---

87 Edmund Burke. 1729 – 1797.

APPENDIX VIII
IN SEARCH OF TRUE INTIMACY

SUPPORTING TEXTS
2 SAMUEL 12: 7-10, 13; GALATIANS 2: 16, 19-21;
LUKE 7: 36 - 8 :3 PSALM 32

We are teaching our daughters to be like this woman…
We are teaching our sons to be like this man.

Bratz Babyz makes a "Babyz Nite Out" doll garbed in fishnet stockings, a hot-pink micromini, and a black leather belt. To look "funalish" (whatever that means), the baby also sports a tummy-flaunting black tank paired with a hot-pink cap. Dare one ask what is planned for "Babyz Nite Out" and what, exactly, she is carrying in her metal-studded purse?…The dolls are officially for ages "four-plus," but they are very popular among two-and three-year-old girls as well.[88]

As I walked around a crowded city shopping area on a hot day last week, it often felt as though glancing anywhere below head-level in any direction was fraught – yet not doing so could clearly result in a twisted ankle. However, amid the plunging necklines and beltlines, piercings and tattoos, one woman stood out. She was wearing a long white summer dress with a red pattern on it, and she stood out because it made her look …pretty! Remember pretty? Ah, yes – I'd almost forgotten it, lost among all the hot, hip, raunchy grrrl-wear that has become the official uniform *de nos jours*.[89]

---

88 Wendy Shalit, *Girls Gone Mild*, (New York: Random House, 2007), xv-xvi.
89 Ibid. 138. The translation of the French idiom is "in our time."

We are teaching our daughters to be like this woman. *A woman known in town to be a sinner…stood behind him [Jesus] at his feet, weeping so that her tears fell upon his feet. Then she wiped them with her hair, kissing them and perfuming them with the oil. When the Pharisee, saw this, he said to himself, "If this man were a prophet, he would know who and what sort of woman this is that touches him – that she is a sinner."*

Twice this woman is labeled as a sinner: by the local people and by this Pharisee. No one forced this woman to be there; no one forced her to bring the expensive perfume; no one forced the kisses. She approached the Savior after a lifetime of searching for him. She searched for him in the things of this world, even though she knew it not. She searched for him in the men she encountered, although he would not be found in their hearts. Finally, she searches for him in a place she fears most…a place where her sins are exposed by the one who owns the house. And she kisses the feet of Christ, perhaps the first kiss she's ever offered out of real love for another. *I tell you, that is why her many sins are forgiven – because of her great love. Little is forgiven the one whose love is small.* And this Pharisee, among others, was one of those who made her the person she was. Only Christ could make her the person she became.

How does this happen? We are teaching our sons to be like *this* man…David. Now David is revered among Jews and Christians alike as the great king. He is legendary both for his trials and triumphs. And yet, David in his day, was responsible for cultivating a lifestyle that objectified women. Thus enters Bathsheba. David with his hundreds of wives and concubines (look it up) still lusted! How is this possible? With hundreds (literally) of women to choose from, David still went after the wife of Uriah.

The Lord says: *I anointed you king of Israel. I rescued you from the hand of Saul. I gave your lord's house and your lord's wives for your own. I gave you the house of Israel and of Judah. And if this were not enough, I could count up for you still more. Why have you spurned the Lord and done evil in his sight? You have cut down Uriah the Hittite with the sword; you took his wife as your own, and him you killed with the sword…* What drives a man to do such a thing?

We could blame society, and should blame society, but that does little to change the state of affairs. We need to begin with our own families...we are the head of the household, the *domestic church*, so it must start there. What happens is so often we get lazy, or tired of fighting the world. I can understand that, believe me. But this culture that promotes the objectification of women, and the emasculation of men through sexual dominance, is made up of people who grew tired of fighting.

We must reclaim our innocence. There is an old wives' tale about how to boil a frog. They say that if you're going to boil a frog, don't heat up the water first. If the water's already boiling, as soon as the frog goes in the pot, he'll hop right out again. Put the frog into the cool water and slowly heat it up to boiling. The frog is not sensitive enough to notice the changing temperature, and will remain there, unaware and boil away. How true is that for us!

The temperature is turned up slowly each year. If you doubt this, just consider what's on television these days. Take any of the shows on television right now, and go back thirty years, even twenty years, and try and put it on the television then. Are you kidding me? It wouldn't happen. There would be such an outcry from the public that the show would immediately be removed. There were times in the sixties when the Church spoke out against certain movies, therefore, people didn't go to see them and very quickly they shut down. No doubt, many of us are boiling and we don't even know it.

Now is a good time to make a moral inventory. How are we living our lives? What kind of model are we setting up for our children, who incidentally, look to us in order to learn how to be adults? What are we allowing them to see and hear? And don't fall into the trap of believing it's enough to regulate what *they* do in your house. We can work very hard to ensure that our household is safe and then allow them to spend time within one that is not safe.

We can no longer depend on a society to regulate shows or movies, and you know this if you've gone to a PG-13 movie lately. In the seventies, the rating would have been "R" or even "X" for some of the current films. We have an obligation to form men who love women for their own sake; who wish to grow in love with them, mind and heart so that one day they might be united in the Sacrament and their union would be complete with a physical consummation. We have an obligation to form men who see the beauty in a woman not as something for him to conquer or possess, but as a gift to be cherished and guarded against malice.

We need to form women who are proud of what they can do with their minds and hearts; who are not so consumed with a sexual body that they starve themselves or allow themselves to be used as they search for love. We have an obligation to teach our sons and daughters how to be Ladies and Gentlemen, in a way that empowers them to one day offer themselves to another as an unspoiled gift. We need to show them what true intimacy is about. And we will do this in a most effective way…when we model the behavior; when we live the lifestyle ourselves. When we live in the way we would want our children to live.

There is another way, and this way applies both to single people, and those who are married. The statements I am about to make are not published anywhere but here, and are based both on our biological make-up and psychological make-up. These statements are based not only on the science, but also the experience of counseling many couples, both married and not married, ages fourteen to forty and beyond.

"Neuroscientists point to numerous current studies that indicate memory involves a set of encoded neural connections that can occur in several parts of the brain. The more powerful the images accompanying an event, the more the brain is stimulated and likely to make it a part of long-term memory."[90] What this means is, the mind records every experience we've ever had, for better or worse. We can't recall this information all the time, except under hypnosis, but the pathways are burned into our memories and therefore have an effect on who we are and who we are becoming. If you doubt this for even a minute, reflect on your first date, with that guy or girl with whom you were madly in "love." Remember what they were wearing? Remember what

---

90 Schacter, Daniel L., *Searching for Memory: The Brain, the Mind, and the Past*, (New York: Basic Books, 1996).

they smelled like (hopefully it was a good scent)? Remember the song playing in the background? These pathways burned through our senses are so strong, that ten years later if we smell that perfume or cologne; or we hear that Peter Cetera song, we are wisped away to that moment years before. True!

Now, scientifically as a species, once we reach puberty our bodies will begin to shout a mantra throughout our body. This mantra composed of urges and chemicals and hormones, etc. is almost overpowering in its demand that we breed! That's right. We are part of the animal kingdom, like it or not, and so the urge is there. We are not like the other animals, however, because we have a soul (I'm not going to debate animal souls here, so move on!). We realize that there is more to life than breeding (most of us do…well some of us do) and that love plays a central role in any relationship. That doesn't mean that such an awareness eliminates all urges or temptations. Those urges stop only later in a process we call death. So our body is shouting that we are *to breed*, while our soul is competing with that mantra desiring a union… these are different.

Bearing in mind these two drives, we proceed with this discussion. We are all seeking intimacy. Intimacy means a communion of persons, a union of the person, mind body and soul, with another. Breeding limits itself to the physical union. Anyone of age has the possibility to breed; I observe in my own life, the tragedy of seeing fourteen and fifteen year old girls pushing their children down the street in a stroller…no man in sight. Children having children. You see, anyone can breed, but not everyone will experience intimacy.

So we have the first date: we get to know the other person, their likes dislikes; plans; dreams; desires. We are becoming one with them in mind and heart. At the end of the night there is a ritual goodnight hug or kiss and the effect is instantaneous. As innocent as that is, the body recognizes this closeness as an antecedent to breeding and as a result, hormones are released, arousal occurs and a pathway is born in the mind.

If the first date was successful, there will be a second. Perhaps a movie is in store this time, so the couple meets, they chat a bit, again getting to know each other in union of mind and heart. During the movie, perhaps one grabs the hand of the other. Certainly this is an innocent enough gesture as well, and yet the mind recognizes this also, as part of the breeding ritual. Hormones are released, arousal occurs and a pathway is made in the mind. At the end of the night, perhaps there is a longer goodnight kiss this time and the same pattern of events lays down a pathway in the mind. Each time something of this nature occurs, the original pathway is strengthened and expanded.

Now, perhaps, the dates have become somewhat more physical. There is deep kissing and inappropriate touching. Each of these stimuli create further pathways, because each time the mind is acknowledging the behavior and essentially saying , "Yes. Now this is what you're *supposed* to be doing. This is part of breeding." And so those pathways will grow deeper and stronger. The communication part of the date has dwindled, because the pathways are so strong. Regardless of the where or when, as the couple gets together, already the mind is thinking "When are we going to do '*it*'." Any other part of the conversation is lost.

What results is disastrous. One day the couple wakes up together, and one looks at the other thinking: "Who is this jerk? I don't even know this person." Sadly, this is not the minority of relationships. Essentially what has happened is that these individuals have "fallen in love" with a body, but the mind and heart become lost. I attribute the high percentage of divorces to this phenomenon. If you doubt this, simply look at the number of couples cohabitating before they marry, if they marry at all. The greatest issue that surfaces in counseling of couples is communication. And I would propose that the communication began to decay as the physical entered into the relationship.

And yet these couples, as incompatible as they are, will remain together sometimes for years. Think about it, how many couples do you know, that have been together for some time, and all they seem to do is fight? Well, why are they together? Because they've given themselves physically to the other, and that makes it very difficult to walk away. Now, what about another scenario.

We go on that first date, and all the same stimuli are present as before. On that first date, during the conversation, it is made clear by our date that she is not going to engage in a physical relationship until after she's married.... "Um...what?!" A little alarm goes off that says, "This is not the *one*. Run away, run away." At that moment, a choice must be made. If this person will not engage with me in a physical relationship, then I need to find someone who will, or...I can stay with her and see what happens. If the person takes a chance and stays with her, then all of a sudden a new pathway is formed in the brain. The remnants of the old are there, and the temptations will still present themselves, however, if they are convicted with the belief that abstinence is the most important thing, the new pathway will predominate.

How does this scenario work out then? Well, the couple gets to know each other in the mind and heart, and if they don't get along, or their differences are too vast, they simply go their separate ways. Nothing is lost. They are not forced to stay in a relationship that they hate; they are not controlled by carnal desire to the point where they do not talk, or begin to keep things from each other. They can be honest.

See, something that is built into our nature (from the animal world) is that if we see the possibility of a physical relationship with another, we will act differently. We will act like the person we think they want us to be. We will try to be cool, or wild, or interested in any number of things. We become the peacock who puffs up and spreads out his tail, or like the lions who show dominance and strength. If there is no possibility of a physical relationship, then there is no reason to act differently around the person. We can be our self.

When two people are in a physical relationship, this is not the case. They will begin to lie, get jealous of the other, mistrust the other and worry whether they are good enough or beautiful enough or sexy enough. The problem is, that the body is finite. The mind and heart are infinite. Think about it. Why is pornography an epidemic, or adult bookstores so abundant and the adult movie franchise a billion dollar business? Because the body gets old when there is nothing more invested. Now notice in this whole treatise, not once did I mention

God, or the Bible, or the Church. And yet, you will find that all three support this theory…because it is how we are made.

We've become a perverted society because we have divorced the sexual act from the sacrament. And if the sexual act is outside of the sacred, then it becomes profane.

We like to see the American flag flying over a neighbor's head, but we do not want to see it under his feet. There is a mystery in that flag; it is more than cloth; it stands for the unseen, the spiritual, for love and devotion to country. The pure are shocked at the impure because of the prostitution of the sacred; it makes the reverent irreverent.[91]

But even within the sacrament of marriage, when couples engage lustfully in the sexual act and reject the possibility of the gift of life, for which we were given our reproductive organs, it also becomes profane. Another reason for the relationship problems and various sexual pathologies is that we have divorced the sexual act from procreation, union, and the good of the couple.

When I meet with couples for marriage preparation, I always ask them two questions: "How do you fight?" (because I want to make sure they do), and "What is the worst thing that could happen in your marriage, short of the death of one of you?" The top two answers to the second question are: Infidelity, and some sort of illness like Parkinson's disease, ALS, etc. Okay…you've just visualized the worst. At this point they usually look at each other and there is an audible "gulp." I want them to focus on those two things as the worst that could happen, because in a few months they will say, "I take you for better or for worse."

If we fall in love with a *body*, then we are destined for disaster, because bodies get old, bodies fail, bodies put on weight and wrinkle. If we fall in love with the heart and mind of the person, then we know, when we look at the other they are the most beautiful person in the world, and that has little to do with their physical appearance. This

---

91 Bishop Fulton Sheen, *The Priest Is Not His Own*, (New York: McGraw-Hill, 1963), 264.

world teaches very clearly that *the body* is the most important thing. It's why we spend billions each year on beauty products and products to keep us young. Some people, I'm convinced, will never decompose once in the grave, because they have preserved themselves so well already, before they're dead.

We cannot fight against this monster, which is the popular society, but we can begin in our own families. We begin in the relationship we have with our spouses, our neighbors, our children. We begin by filtering the garbage our brain is exposed to every day. We begin by dressing ourselves modestly when the moment calls for it, and making sure our children do the same. We begin, when we see past the exterior, that the world holds so high, and into the heart of the person, as Jesus did. And we pray, please Lord, allow me to see others as You see them. In that world...then...there will be no place for the "Bratz dolls", or the movies, books, or magazines that are labeled "Adult" because we will be true adults, the ones who are models for those who have not yet lost their innocence.

APPENDIX IX
RETREAT

Retreat to St. Vincent Seminary

Why can't a retreat ever be uneventful? I had chosen to take my motorcycle out to Latrobe for my retreat. I was hoping the weather would be nice, as there are many wonderful views out there among the rolling hills of western Pennsylvania. I had taken the turnpike for part of the trip and it was beginning to rain as I neared my exit in Bedford.

All of a sudden the bike jerked in one direction. I was traveling at least sixty-five miles per hour, and I shudder to think what would have happened had I not been alert. I leaned a bit to correct the balance and again, the bike jerked. It was raining, and the bike was off balance. Could these Pennsylvania roads really be this bad? I had just passed a semi, and was pulling into the right lane, when the bike jerked to one side and then to the other. What was going on? What was wrong? And then I heard it! Something hit the road and as I looked in my side mirror, to my horror, my carry-on bag was tumbling down the highway. The semi braked and ran over top of it. It was as though the carry-on was eaten by this beast behind me.

I pulled over quickly, the bike still in fifth gear, and hit the kill switch. The truck had regained control and pulled over behind me. The trucker was very apologetic as he told me he ran over my suitcase, draggin' it for about a hundred yards. All I could think of was the accident that was almost caused by me. I asked where it was and he said, still back in the road. I ran east as fast as I could, bounding past the semi on the bank, and saw my carry-on in the center lane, and then something else. It was my breviary, spinning on the road like a disk someone had just hurled amidst the traffic.

As I approached the place where the breviary was, traffic slowed and I dashed out and retrieved the book. The people seemed confused, but I quickly darted out and brought back the carry-on as well. Traffic was still slowing, and then I noticed my Birkenstocks flipping around like fish out of water, as cars continue to flow past. I waited for a break, and then darted out a third time and got both sandals, which I am wearing as I write this. And then it hit me. On top of my carry-on was my laptop, with this book and many other files. It must have been vaporized, because I didn't see pieces of plastic or material anywhere. It was in a case, and I had stuffed my calendar in there too, but where was the case?

The trucker approached me. "You all right?" he said, obviously noticing the look on my face. It was a look that said, "I almost died" or "I almost caused an accident" or "I almost..." "There's something hanging from the back of your motorcycle," he said. I glanced in the direction of his gaze, and hanging by the strap was the laptop case. The case was hanging by a thread (literally), and the handle had been torn by the wheel. I brought all the contents back to the bike, and the trucker, convinced that I was okay, took off. And then I saw it. The tie-down I had used popped its spring and the strap came loose. When it did, it wound in the back wheel, which is what had thrown the bike around so much. There was so much heat that the plastic and vinyl melted. A whole chain of events which might have changed my life forever...but did I mention...it was Divine Mercy Sunday.

I'm typing on the laptop now; wearing my sandals, and will pray *Night Prayer* from my Breviary. Sure the leather cover is torn and road-burned, but I am untouched...the trucker untouched, and all who witnessed it will tell of the poor guy who lost his luggage; I will tell of the mercy of God. Such mercy as to suspend the laws of physics, just for a moment, so that I might *retreat*.

BIBLIOGRAPHY

Benedict XVI. *Sacramentum Caritatis.* Vatican City: Libreria Editrice Vaticana, 2006.

Brueggemann, Walter. *The Prophetic Imagination.* Fortress Press, 1978.

DeMello, Rev. Anthony, S.J. *The Way to Love.* New York: Doubleday, 1992.

Enhanced Strong's Lexicon, (Oak Harbor, WA: Logos Research Systems, Inc., 1995), *Lutron.*

Gregory the Great. *Homily on the Gospels* (26, 7-9: PL 76, 1201-1202) in The Liturgy of the Hours, Vol. III. New York: Catholic Book Publishing Company, 1975.

Hahn, Scott. *A Father Who Keeps His Promises: God's Covenant Love in Scripture.* Ann Arbor Michigan: Servant Publications, 1998.

Ilibagiza, Immaculae. *Left To Tell: Discovering God Amidst the Rwandan Holocaust.* California: Hay House, 2007.

John Paul II, *Holy Thursday Letters To My Brother Priests,* Edited by James P. Socias. Chicago: Midwest Theological Forum, 1992.

Kollar, Charles Allen. *Solution-Focused Pastoral Counseling: An Effective Short-Term Approach for Getting People Back on Track.* Grand Rapids, MI: Zondervan, 1997.

L'Amour, Louis. *Lonely on the Mountain.* New York: Bantam Books.

Lewis, C. S. *A Grief Observed.* New York: Bantam Books, 1976.

_____. *Letters of C.S. Lewis.* Ed. By W. H. Lewis. London: Geoffrey Bles, 1966.

_____. *Mere Christianity*. San Francisco: Harper, 1972.

Ratzinger, Joseph Cardinal. *Images of Hope: Meditations on Major Feasts*. San Francisco: Ignatius Press, 2006.

Rolheiser, Rev. Ronald, OMI., *Against the Infinite Horizon: The Finger of God in Our Everyday Lives*. New York: Crossroad Publishing Company, 2001.

Schacter. Daniel L. *Searching for Memory: The Brain. the Mind. and the Past*. New York: Basic Books, 1996.

Shalit, Wendy. *Girls Gone Mild*. New York: Random House, 2007.

Sheen. Fulton J. *Life of Christ*. New York: Image Books, 1977.

_____. *Lift Up Your Hearts*. New York: McGraw-Hill, 1950.

_____. *Peace of Soul*. New York: McGraw-Hill, 1949.

_____. *The Priest is not His Own*. New York: McGraw-Hill, 1963.

Sparks, T. A., in Charles Allen Kollar. *Solution-Focused Pastoral Counseling: An Effective Short-Term Approach for Getting People Back on Track*. Grand Rapids, MI: Zondervan, 1997.

Strubel, Anthony W. and Michael W. Rothan. *Home Free,* Indiana: IUniverse Publishers, 2009.

Saint Theresa of Avila. *Interior Castle*. Translated and Edited by E. Allison Peers. New York: Doubleday Press, 1989.

Thompson, William M., The Struggle for Theology's Soul: Contesting Scripture in Christology. New York: The Crossroad Publishing Company, 1996.

Van Breeman, Rev. Peter. *Called by Name*. New Jersey: Dimension Books, 1976.

_____. *Certain as the Dawn*. New Jersey: Dimension Books, 1980.

_____. *The God Who Won't Let Go.* Notre Dame. IN: Ave Maria Press, 2001.

Vianney, Saint Jean-Marie. in *The Cure D'Ars: St. Jean-Marie-Baptiste Vianney.* by Abbe Francis Trochu. Rockford Ill: Tan Books and Publishers. Inc., 1977.

West, Christopher. *Theology of the Body Explained.* Pauline Books and Media, 2007.

Breinigsville, PA USA
07 March 2010
233745BV00005B/1/P